Life, Love, and Laughter

Praise for Life, Love and Laughter

What he has written is much more than a collection of personal memories. It is a remarkably interesting and delightful memoir of our country Canada from 1915 to the present time.

He has put together a series of his activities and observations which are a delight to know and a happy introduction to our future. A perfect reading from time to time, for those of us of senior years, and especially for the coming generation of young Canadians.

The Honourable John A. Fraser
Former Member of Parliament and Cabinet Minister

A charming collection of memories and musings that conveys the author's lively curiosity, keen sense of humour and joie de vivre.

John Ellis has influenced many business leaders through his philanthropy and personal leadership. In sharing these stories, he offers further insight into a life well-lived. His example is instructive for all of us who wish to enjoy a full and productive life.

Barb Martineau
Senior Associate Director, Advancement
Beedie School of Business | Simon Fraser University

This book is great fun to read and it reminds us of how to live well throughout one's life. Personally and professionally, John Ellis is abundantly successful, and a true gentleman. His secrets are in the stories told here.

Jack Blaney, OBC
President Emeritus, Simon Fraser University

John Ellis has lived a long and rich life. In his book *Life, Love and Laughter*, John gives us a range of stories — including a couple of fascinating ones describing his time in London in 1940 and Holland towards the end of the second world war, and musings on subjects ranging from tea to water to the longevity of the Japanese. It is a book that will inform and amuse, and is a very good read.

Damien McGoldrick
Executive Director, Crofton Manor by Revera

Life, Love and Laughter

A. John Ellis

GRANVILLE ISLAND
PUBLISHING

The contents of this book are a collection of writings done by the author throughout the years at different stages of his life. Some written by others are also included.

Library and Archives Canada Cataloguing in Publication

Ellis, A. John, author
    Life, love and laughter / A. John Ellis.

ISBN 978-1-926991-68-9 (paperback)

    1. Ellis, A. John. 2. Bankers—Canada—Biography. I. Title.

HG1552.E46A3 2016   332.1092   C2016-905478-0
ISBN: 978-1-926991-68-9

Book designer: Omar Gallegos

Granville Island Publishing Ltd.
212 – 1656 Duranleau St. Granville Island
Vancouver, BC, Canada V6H 3S4

604-688-0320 / 1-877-688-0320
info@granvilleislandpublishing.com
www.granvilleislandpublishing.com

*Dedicated to
all the members of
the Ellis clan*

Table of Contents

Prologue

by A. John Ellis

Having been a writer of numerous short stories and articles, I decided a compilation of such items would make a more interesting read than an autobiography. Now in my 101st year, I believe members of my clan might find this book illuminating in that the items illustrate some of my thinking over the many years.

I must admit that good luck has played a major role in my life. For instance, having been a flying member of the Montreal Light Aeroplane Club, I was accepted for flying training with a Pilot Officer's commission in September of 1939. I was delighted and excited with the prospect and was all set to go, having passed a medical exam, but my father intervened, contending the war would last only six months and I would probably be killed and nobody would thank me. I bowed to his forceful wishes but made a pact with him that if the war was still on in six months, I would join up. So after six months, I applied to the RCAF, only to find I would be accepted but with a non-commissioned rank. In the time spent waiting, I had qualified as an army officer by taking a COTC course at McGill University. So I joined a regiment as a first lieutenant. During the Battle of Britain, fighter pilots lasted only 17 hours of flying time and I would probably have been one of them. Thank you, dad!

My second good luck story was to have met, courted and married my wonderful wife in England in 1943, followed by 67 years of happy marriage. The third good luck item was to have been temporarily on duty in Canada when D-Day was launched on the French coast with heavy casualties. A fourth piece of good luck was to have survived the balance of WWII without mishap in the face of heavy fighting.

It is not unreasonable to believe that an unusually good primary education at Lower Canada College in Montreal allowed me to obtain employment in 1933 by the Bank of Montreal as a junior at the Park & Bernard branch in that city — this during the terrible "dirty thirties". I must add that I have a deep appreciation for LCC because of its excellence in tuition and social awareness instilled over the years. I believe this superior education was what made me one of the only three male hires in Canada by BMO during the depression.

The school's excellent motto is "Non Nobis Solum", which can be interpreted as "Not by Ourselves Alone". Me and several of my colleagues have lived by this motto.

My banking career was of course interrupted by five years fighting for freedom, during which time the bank assured all concerned that a job awaited us when the war was over. And they kept their word.

After the war, a slow climb up the executive ladder commenced, culminating many years later in an offer of the presidency of the bank, which I declined with much regret as I did not wish to disturb myself or my family by leaving British Columbia where our roots had taken a strong hold. I retired as Vice Chairman of the bank and I am still an honourary director of the bank with pleasant memories of that grand institution and of Lower Canada College as well.

Both those fine institutions undoubtedly enabled me to carve out a business/community career, which encompassed some thirty-six national and global companies and community organizations either as chairman or director involving a great deal of worldwide travel and education.

I am eternally grateful to my late wife who was always by my side helping and advising me while running the domestic side of life and chiefly raising the children. In our later years, she and I travelled about one million miles worldwide promoting Canada business-wise and culturally.

I can say with all certainty in my heart that I have lived a wonderful and fulfilling life.

Acknowledgements

I very much appreciate the expert and experienced guidance of Jo Blackmore, who is the publisher of Granville Island Publishing. She and her team have done a great job.

My thanks also to Ms. Anji Lowe, who did a grand job of the essential typing.

A tip of the hat to Mr. Mardi Lee for his expert photography and guidance.

Thanks too, to my daughter Mrs. Susan Hoch, who always stood ready to offer her valued opinion with patience and understanding.

Also, to my son Robert, whose guidance was much appreciated.

I am also indebted to my remarkable doctor G.B. Ryder, a retired MD who practices Integrative Medicine with outstanding results in diagnosing and prescribing for everyday ailments. I know he has saved my life several times, and has encouraged me to continue working on this book whenever I have felt too unwell to continue.

For Starters 1915–1938

Flashbacks and Reflections

by A. John Ellis

There is a school of thought, which contends that to live longer and happier, one should live for the day, plan for the future and forget the past. Another group says that's rubbish — the past made us what we are and it's beneficial to reminisce about our erstwhile achievements, failures and other significant activities. Both sides have their points but it is quite possible to pay heed to the here and now, plan for the future and muse about the past all at the same time, which a lot of us do.

Personally, I have in my memory an assortment of what I call 'flashbacks' and 'reflections' that intrude in my thinking from time to time. It is reasonable to believe that every one of advanced years has a collection of memories that could provide a wealth of themes for many a book. But alas, such material for the most part is never shown publicly. Here and there, a few who have experiences they feel other people would like to know about, produce autobiographies hoping for high-volume book sales and some go into print mainly for the benefit of their families. Most people lead unspectacular lives but at the same time have stored up a number of real-life unforgettable, but often trivial vignettes. I belong to such a group and the following is necessarily a small selection of my reflections of the years immediately after WWI and before WWII.

My first flashback is appropriately categorized and has more or less pinpointed for me the dawning of my intelligence. It was in New York City in 1918; I was three years of age and prone to experimentation as are most denizens of that age group. We — my parents, four sisters, and myself — were living in an apartment overlooking Central Park. I can picture the apartment, the impressive coloured gentleman who pulled ropes to activate the elevator and the view of the park from our windows. One day, with experimentation uppermost in my mind, I placed a lead soldier in an empty light socket and turned it on. The result was electrifying to say the least — a brilliant flash and bang that blackened my face and hand but fortunately was otherwise benign. Electricity 101: my first lesson in elementary electricity is as vivid today as it was 85 years ago!

The same year, at the New York Zoo, I was in front of a lion's den hanging on to the cage bars when a huge lion ambled up to within spitting distance of me, opened wide his cavernous mouth, complete with large menacing fangs, and let out an almighty roar. This gave me a frightful scare and I have never forgotten the episode. It cured me forever of wanting to go on an African Safari.

In 1919, the great international influenza epidemic was raging and causing countless deaths. By that time, we had moved to Montreal and were living near a thoroughfare leading to the cemeteries at the back of Mount Royal. Steady processions of horse-drawn carts carrying coffins, en route to the cemeteries, continued for weeks. One afternoon, I was playing in the front garden when an automobile drew up, a doctor alighted and he asked me if he could use our telephone. In my innocence, I happily led him into the house — doors were never locked in those days — to my mother's consternation as she realized he had probably been attending flu victims and would be a germ carrier. She was right, as shortly afterwards the whole family and domestic staff contracted the dreaded disease. Happily, all recovered with no side effects. Except for me — I was given a stern lecture about the dangers of fraternizing with total strangers and made to feel very guilty. It probably was a good lesson.

Most readers will be familiar with the 'Roaring Twenties', with emphasis on varying aspects of the era such as the tremendous boost given to freedom of expression, the fast-track development of industry, the runaway speculation on the equity markets, the 'flapper' age, or a variety of other vastly changed aspects of society engendered to some extent by the relief experienced from the realization that the Great War — heralded as the war to end all wars — was over.

To a small boy surrounded by four much older sisters, I was vaguely aware of the much publicized flapper antics of the twenties. Bobbed hair, short skirts, turned-down hose, powdered knees, cigarette smoking using long black silver-trimmed holders, heavy make-up, the jazz age, the Charleston, and whatnot. The flappers offended the older generations because they defied the conventions of hitherto acceptable feminine behaviour. All this activity was of little or no concern to a youngster like me as I made my way through the decade.

One insignificant twenties-era vignette that has stuck with me was a memorable fishing trip with a member of the British Empire Tuna Team off Shelburne, Nova Scotia in an area called Soldier's Rip where, after an exciting struggle, he boated an 800-pound tuna. I was presented with the unfortunate tuna's eyeball, which I prized for some time, using it as a magnifying glass until it eventually shriveled and became opaque.

During the twenties, I became very 'air-minded', building and flying myriad model airplanes and reading every account about the exploits of the WWI air aces I could lay my hands on, including the famous German fighter pilot Manfred von Richtofen, the 'Red Baron'. My Canadian heroes were, of course, Billy Bishop, credited with destroying 72 enemy aircrafts, Ray Collishaw with 60, and Maclaren with 53. Little thought was given to the downed enemy pilots — just the overwhelming glamour and excitement of it all. I couldn't wait to grow up and become airborne, but it wasn't until the mid-thirties that the desire became reality as I became a flying member of the Montreal Light Aeroplane Club.

It was the era of trans-Atlantic flight attempts. The first successful flight was made by Captain John Alcock and Lieutenant Arthur Brown flying a WWI Vickers Vimy Bomber who, on June 15th, 1919 flew from St. John's, Newfoundland to Galway, Ireland, there landing in a bog. Elapsed time was 16 hours and 12 minutes.

The trans-Atlantic flight, which captured worldwide attention and changed the future of aviation forever was made by Charles Augustus Lindbergh on May 20–21, 1927. At the helm of the *Spirit of St. Louis*, a fragile single-engine, high-wing airplane, he flew non-stop from Roosevelt Field — near New York — to Paris, 3,610 miles in 34 hours.

Overnight, he became an international hero and the most famous man in the world. The *Spirit of St. Louis* hangs in the atrium of the National Air and Space Museum in Washington, D.C. It is worth a visit. Volumes have been written about this determined man and the impact he made on aviation. I had never been more excited about an event than when I was tracking, through the media, his remarkable historic flight. It irrevocably sealed my intense interest in flying.

The end of the decade brought about the start of economic disaster, virtually worldwide, triggered by the US stock market crash known as 'Black Tuesday', October 29th, 1929. When the equity market had peaked in September of that year, it is said that some 40% of stock market values had nothing to back the prices. Such artificially high prices were bid up simply because speculators believed there would be no end to rising prices. Stocks were being bought on only a 10% margin and speculation by unsophisticated gamblers was rampant. The bubble burst and the US Federal Reserve was powerless to stabilize the chaotic situation. The resulting confusion in the US saw many bank failures in the early thirties, notably after a second stock market crash in 1931, and there was tremendous hardship everywhere.

I was acutely aware of the troubles as my father was in the investment business and was seriously affected. The election of President Franklin Delano Roosevelt in November 1932 in the USA had a stabilizing effect. In his inaugural address, he endeavoured to reassure the world with the now-famous phrase "the only thing we have to fear is fear itself." His subsequent actions and the outbreak of WWII finally brought about the return to economic prosperity.

One aspect of life in North America that is worthy of reflection was the enactment of the National Prohibition Act (also referred to as the Volstead Act) in the USA. Introduced in 1920, with the lofty ideals of making the population sensible and sober, it had the opposite effect and public opinion forced its repeal on December 5th, 1933, due to the accelerating and serious criminal behaviour that followed, which seemed unstoppable. Under the act, beer, wine and other intoxicating malt or vinous liquors, were limited to one half of 1% alcohol content by volume. This, of course, shut down the beer, wine and distilling industries in the United States. Canada did not adopt prohibition so, consequently, alcohol production and rum-running from the Atlantic to the Pacific oceans — across the lengthy unguarded border — flourished in a highly profitable manner. During prohibition in the US, the criminal element soon had control of the rum-running and the illicit outlets known as 'speakeasies' of which there were thousands across the country — in 1925, one estimate for New York City alone put the figure as high as 100,000. Bullets flew, assassinations and murders were commonplace amongst the criminal gangs and the situation was largely out of control. Prohibition just would not work, proving once again that denying freedom of choice for what is viewed as a harmless pastime causes the masses eventually to revolt, meanwhile finding ways to flaunt the law.

The 'Dirty Thirties' were aptly named as people struggled to survive. There was very heavy unemployment everywhere but, somehow or other, the majority of the population got through this rather desperate period, if often aided by government make-work programs, breadlines and soup kitchens. The economy began to improve towards the end of the decade and as mentioned, the outbreak of WWII started things humming again.

The basic lessons learned from the '29 and '31 crashes, followed by the hardships experienced in the thirties, have stood me in very good stead and have influenced my investment and economic decisions ever since. Young people today have, of course, missed such experiences and often are understandably bewildered when the economy takes an unexpected downward plunge, as it will from time to time, ad infinitum.

I'll conclude by quoting from an editorial in *Harper's Magazine*, which was headed "The Worst of Times" and reads as follows:

> "It's a gloomy moment in the history of our country. Not in the lifetime of most men has there been so much grave and deep apprehension; never has the future seemed so incalculable as at this time. The domestic situation is in chaos. Our dollar is weak throughout the world. Prices are so high as to be utterly impossible. The political cauldron

seethes and bubbles with uncertainty. Russia hangs as usual, like a cloud, dark and silent upon the horizon. It is a solemn moment. Of our troubles, no man can see the end."

This appeared in *Harper's Magazine* in 1847 A.D. — 156 years ago!

Quod erat demonstrandum.

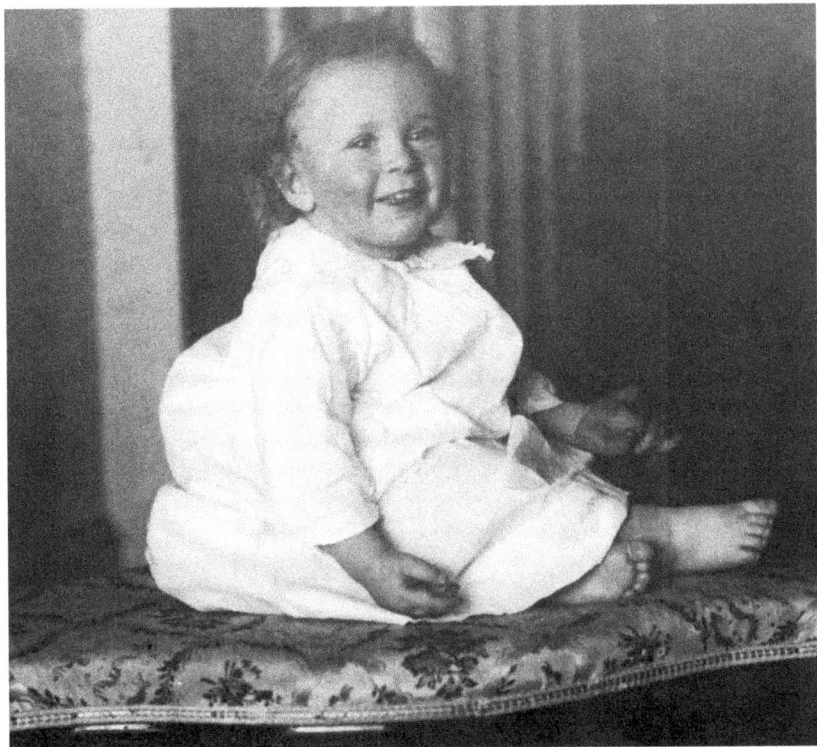

Alfred John Ellis. One year old in Montreal.

John flanked by his father and grandfather. Fishing trip circa 1924.

John's four sisters. Margery in front and in descending order on the back are Ernestine, Frances and Audrey.

The Ellis family in Montreal, 1923. John is on the far left; in the back is sister Margery and two family friends. In the front are mother and father.

John is in the middle of the second row with the BMO English rugby team out of Montreal, which competed with Glace Bay miners in Cape Breton, Nova Scotia, 1938. Even though they were trounced, they came back to play on the same cinder field the next year. John experienced much ribbing because he appeared in protective long johns.

Tales of World War II
1939–1945

Formal portrait of John soon after enlisting. Montreal, 1940.

Our Debt to the RAF

by A. John Ellis

Armistice . . . what does it mean to you?

For many people, it signifies that most precious factor: *freedom*. Freedom to pursue our lives and activities in any way we wish. Freedom of choice in everything that comprises our lifestyles.

During the Second World War, at the dictates of a power-hungry madman, most of Europe had been enslaved and deprived of freedom by the invading armed forces. In the early days of WWII, England was the last remaining haven of democratic freedom, suffering a terrific battering from a powerful Luftwaffe, opposed by a small group of RAF pilots flying Spitfires and Hurricanes, fortunately backed up by a remarkable radar communications system and an ability to break the enemy's message code.

The situation was very tense for the civilian population and our fighting forces alike. That famous statesman

Churchill, in one of his wondrous speeches, stated that never before in history had so many owed so much to so few, referring of course to that small heroic group of RAF pilots. It's reminiscent of the David and Goliath legend and it set me thinking about how freedom was achieved in those terrible days. Undoubtedly, our Western world owes it to those pilots who were able to beat all odds and not only defeated a very powerful air force, but were able to hold the fort until adequate reinforcements arrived in the form of a well-equipped US Air Force.

I was an officer in Le Régiment de Maisonneuve of Montreal and our unit had just arrived in England in the late summer of 1940 after sailing from Halifax, Nova Scotia in convoy, and arriving at a Scottish port. There, a train awaited us for transport to Aldershot, England. It was a beautiful, clear, and sunny day and our train had been put into a sideline just outside of London to allow a fast priority train to pass us. There, we had a front-row view of a raging aerial dogfight above London.

I have a vivid recollection of hearing the rattle of machine-gun fire and watching aircraft fall out of the sky — some on fire — and pilots with or without parachutes, trying to escape the battle. I remember thinking to myself, "Those poor young men on both sides trying to kill each other," but that was where the fight for freedom began. I wondered what the young and heroic pilots were thinking. I found a bit of an answer in mentioning one young pilot.

John Gillespie Magee, aged 19 years, was killed on December 11th, 1941. Besides doing his duty chasing the enemy and firing the eight machine guns of his fighter, he had much finer thoughts in mind. In his spare and rare time, he composed the following poem, heralding inspiring flying thoughts:

Oh! I have slipped the surly bonds of Earth
And danced the skies on laughter-silvered wings;
Sunward I've climbed, and joined the tumbling mirth
Of sun-split clouds, — and done a hundred things
You have not dreamed of — wheeled and soared and swung
High in the sunlit silence. Hov'ring there,
I've chased the shouting wind along, and flung
My eager craft through footless halls of air...

Up, up the long, delirious burning blue
I've topped the wind-swept heights with easy grace
Where never lark, or ever eagle flew —
And, while with silent, lifting mind I've trod
The high untrespassed sanctity of space,
Put out my hand, and touched the face of God.

The average life expectancy of the Battle of Britain pilots was 17 flying hours. What a terrible shame, but the fight for freedom started with them. John's poem brings tears to my eyes every time I read it.

Blithe Spirits
and Gloomy Times

by A. John Ellis

Hail to thee, blithe Spirit!
Bird thou never wert,
That from Heaven, or near it,
Pourest thy full heart
In profuse strains of unpremeditated art.

(Opening verse of "To a Skylark"
by Percy Bysshe Shelley)

This and many more of the best poems in the English language can be found in the delightful little books known as *Palgrave's Golden Treasury* (officially *The Golden Treasury of English Songs and Lyrics*, edited by Francis Turner Palgrave). I have a copy of Book IV, which I particularly treasure as the inside cover of it has the following handwritten message:

To: Captain John Ellis, Canadian Army
From: Lt R.W. Keep, 2/Commando

Hoping these few gems of the English tongue will
help in the difficult task of civilizing that barren
state across the pond!!!!
(any remarks?)
                                                    29th January 1943

And thereby hangs a rather poignant and true story of a chance and strong but fleeting friendship.

It was in England. England and indeed the Western World, had been saved from being subjugated by a power-mad *régime* led by a maniacal dictator, only because of a small group of gallant young men flying Spitfire and Hurricane fighter aircraft, a great statesman who inspired an indomitable race of patriotic people, and a huge tactical blunder by the enemy. Hitler and Göring had thought the Royal Air Force could be wiped from the sky, and with its failing, the English population could be bombed into submission. They were wrong on both counts. The strategic situation had very materially improved with the mighty United States of America now in the conflict and at last there was a glimmer of light at the end of the tunnel. Victory for the Allies seemed assured in the desert and the Italian campaign had yet to commence.

While the Allied navies and air forces were heavily engaging the enemy during the early forties, in England, the ground forces saw no action except for the disastrous Dieppe Raid in 1942 and some commando forays on German installations on the French coast. The Dieppe force was approximately 6,000 strong, of which 4,963 were Canadians. Only 2,210 of those managed to get back to England, 907 lost their lives, 1,946 were captured and 3,367 were wounded. The balance of the special force, which also suffered heavy losses, was comprised of British commandos and a few American rangers. There was strong air support by the RAF and the RCAF as well as strong Royal Navy support. The raid produced a tremendous air battle. The RAF lost 106 aircraft — more than any other day of the war — and the RCAF lost 13 aircraft. The navy lost one destroyer. Much more could be said but, in summary, the raid plan was widely criticized as being poorly conceived with little accruing benefit. The proponents claim that it was a disastrous introduction to real warfare for our Canadians.

The thousands of Canadian ground troops, many of which had been stationed in England for over three years, were anxious to get into action and were becoming more than restless. Keeping up morale was a priority for the senior commanders and, consequently, ongoing tactical exercises and simulated battle conditions were the orders of the day, combined with formal learning courses covering a wide cross-section of army life and fighting requirements. As an aside, from the troops' point of view, chasing English girls was their real priority. A story making the rounds was that a jilted and angry Canadian fiancée wrote from Canada demanding to know what the English girls had that she, and others like her, didn't have. The answer came back smartly — "Nothing, but they have it over here!" The result of our troops' priority was that there were 44,886 war brides by December 31st, 1946. Other countries accounted for an additional

2,897 war brides — with Holland in the lead with 1,886 brides. A real Canadian achievement!

I met Lt. R.W. Keep through a formal learning course, I recall. At the time, I was a Brigade Intelligence Officer. The brigadier had called me into his office one day.

"Ellis," he said, "we want you to attend a course on German intelligence being conducted at Cambridge University."

I said I had already taken that course at Cambridge some months ago, but he assured me it couldn't be the same as it had a different number. Who was I to argue? So off I went, only to be confronted by the course chief instructor. He recognized me and stated the course was identical to the one I had already taken. Fortunately, he had a good sense of humour and was understanding, saying that as long as I reported in daily at some time, I could otherwise do as I pleased for the next three weeks. Lt. Keep, another course candidate, was also accorded the same privilege. We quickly got together and decided to meet daily for sightseeing and pub-crawling. What a wonderful location for such pleasant activity. The University of Cambridge is one of the oldest in the world and one of the largest in the United Kingdom. It is comprised of many colleges, some of which were founded as early as the thirteenth century and steeped in tradition — a paradise for sightseeing and a far cry from learning to kill or be killed.

My new friend and I found many areas of mutual interest besides the fascinating sightseeing. For instance, in sports, we had both been the scrum half for our respective rugger teams. In things academic, we enjoyed languages, particularly Latin. In music, we enjoyed the popular classics, Cole Porter and the big bands. We shared a delight in the poetry of R. Browning, Burns, Keats, Kipling, Shelley, Wordsworth and others. We decided Shelley's "To a Skylark" best suited our present and unexpected break in an otherwise unpleasant and dangerous existence. We were two blithe melodious songs of "unpremeditated art" in the skies above. After a few days of almost continuous note comparing, we decided that, after the war, we would explore England and Canada. In the meantime, we would take our leaves together and roam the Hebrides for starts. We mostly avoided discussing the war, although Keep did volunteer some information about his commando training and actions — really a kill-or-be-killed existence. I gathered that small highly-trained task forces would infiltrate enemy installations on the French coast in the dead of night, destroy the targets and quickly withdraw, taking no prisoners. I understood he had participated in more than one successful operation but, for security reasons, did not press him for details.

Like all good things, this pleasant interlude came to an end and we parted company vowing to keep in touch. A few days after my arrival back at Brigade Headquarters, I found the copy of *Palgraves's Golden Treasury* awaiting me with the facetious and challenging note inscribed. For the next month or two, we exchanged notes until one day, I did not receive a reply.

I later learned he had been killed in action. Something had gone awry and my friend had succumbed to the second half of kill-or-be-killed. I can only hope he is in heaven or "near it", as Shelley wrote, and soaring with the skylarks.

Love During the Blitz

by A. John Ellis

The admirers of *South Pacific*, which is still being shown in spite of its age because of its excellence, will recall the wonderful songs. These include the biggest hit of any Rodgers and Hammerstein musical, the opening verse of which is as follows:

> *Some enchanted evening*
> *You may see a stranger*
> *You may see a stranger*
> *Across a crowded room*
> *And somehow you know*
> *You know even then*
> *That somewhere you'll see her*
> *Again and again*

The lyrics go on to suggest premonitions can't be analyzed and wise men do not try, but when a true love has been found, never let her go. It's a heart-warming story, developed in a most romantic setting, but the majority of viewers, maybe with tears in their eyes, probably shrug their shoulders and say it's delightful theatre but really not realistic, that there is no place in our lives for such romantic drivel. I beg to differ with such people because, while the setting was far removed from a lovely palm-treed and relaxed location, the whole scenario fitted my 1943 experience in England when towns and cities — particularly London — were being bombed nightly and set on fire with heavy human casualties.

I was an unmarried 28-year-old Canadian army officer when, one day, my best army friend phoned me from Alton Hants, where he was running a company commanders course while I was located forty miles distant. He invited me to a dance in Alton, where there would be a group of nurses attending from a local hospital. I accepted. I learned subsequently that the nurses were reluctant to accept because Canadian soldiers were considered to be too rough a bunch, but their matron insisted they accept, saying the boys had volunteered to come a long way to join the fight for freedom and the least the RN's could do would be to spend a few hours socializing with them.

I arrived at the dance a little late and dancing was in full swing. I looked at the couples and, suddenly, I felt something like a jolt of lightning, because there in the middle of the floor was a pretty young nurse and her partner. Like most unattached men of my age group, I had in my imaginative mind's eye the girl of my dreams and there she was — exactly like in my dream! I could hardly believe it, but I said to myself: "There's the girl

I'm going to marry," even though we had never met. Pulling rank, I cut in on the couple and spent the rest of the evening with her, chatting and comparing notes. We seemed to have a lot in common and I hoped and prayed we could meet again. Her name was Joan, an RN planning to become an MD. She had no idea I had romantic visions, but she said she would be happy to see me again.

I was convinced I had met my lifetime soul mate and lover, but I took heed of the sage in *South Pacific*, who had said, "once you have met her, never let her go." Good advice, but it was not simple, particularly in war-torn England in 1943.

However, I was determined to overcome all obstacles. So, I set about hoping to win her heart by courting her whenever possible with a barrage of luncheons, dinners, picnics, movies and other social events of a getting-to-know-you nature. After several meetings, I detected that she was perhaps becoming more interested in me. Then an incident occurred, one that was unusual and challenging.

It was on a Sunday night when I had taken her to dinner in London when, to our horror, we found we had missed the last train back to Alton. A little research found that there was a train, which would take us within five miles of Alton. Joan was absolutely frantic, as she felt if she didn't report back to the hospital by midnight, her good reputation would be ruined. I knew the countryside and said I could get her back if she were willing to hike the five miles cross-country. She readily agreed to undertake the arduous venture.

So, we set out. The sky was a deep and dark clear blue, twinkling star-studded, with a heavy dew falling.

Nearby Portsmouth was being bombed, on fire with an aerial battle underway and aircraft falling out of the sky. Quite a backdrop for a lovers' hike! At one point, we rested under a farmer's haystack holding hands and watching the Portsmouth raid. But even with time for rest, we finally got back to the hospital before zero hour.

I believe it was the hike and some later advice from Joan's aunt and mentor that "good men don't grow on trees," meaning me, that allowed me to pop the question. We were married on the 6th of October, 1943. I was due to return to Canada to attend a course at the Royal Military College in November, and we were lucky enough to arrange to have Joan accompany me on a great and fast ship that outmanoeuvred all U-boats from Liverpool to Halifax because of her speed.

Following the RMC course, I stayed on instructing. Joan joined me, living most enjoyably in a Kingston rental apartment until I was returned by air to the fighting in Europe. During my absence, she resumed nursing at the Royal Victoria Hospital in Montreal. Happily, in 1945, I returned safely and resumed my business career. Joan became a very good artist; working in oils, and latterly, joined me travelling over one million miles promoting Canada culturally and businesswise throughout the world.

1943 was undoubtedly my finest year, and our marriage was a great one with 67 years of happiness and resulting today in three successful children, ten grandchildren and five, going on six, great-grandchildren.

At over 100 years of age, I feel very lucky although, sadly, my wonderful partner in life passed away in 2010.

A Memorable Night in Belgium

by A. John Ellis

It was late 1944 and prospects for the Allies were improving. We had come a long way since the sinister days of Dunkirk when German victory seemed imminent but almost miraculously was not to be — due largely to Hitler's misguided strategy.

The bloody battles on the beaches and across Normandy, where many of my friends and regimental colleagues had been killed or wounded, had been won at great cost in men and equipment. Caen had finally fallen and the enemy forces were retreating steadily towards their homeland. We already had gained air supremacy, our navies had control of the vital Atlantic shipping lanes and, on the ground in Europe, we were enjoying a bit of a breather, although we were not complacent, believing the enemy to have lots of fight left in him.

After being stationed in England from 1940 to 1943, I returned to Canada in late 1943 to take a War Staff Course at the Royal Military College in Kingston,

Ontario. This was followed by a session there as an instructor. Consequently, and in retrospect luckily, I had missed a lot of heavy action following D-Day. Happily, my English wife, Joan, was permitted to emigrate and accompanied me to Canada, travelling from Liverpool to Halifax, Nova Scotia on the *RMS Mauretania*. At that time, German U-boat activity was at its peak, but that splendid ship's great speed allowed us to zigzag our way to Halifax unescorted and without incident.

Joan and I enjoyed about a year together away from the war zone but, due to heavy staff officer losses in France, our military authorities became concerned that a shortage of trained staff officers was developing and, along with several others, I was recalled without notice, flown back to England and subsequently sent to France and Belgium.

In late 1944, I found myself in the thick of it, at a Canadian Army Headquarters in Belgium acting as a jack-of-all-trades Liaison Officer while awaiting a posting. One of my first assignments was to try to locate a platoon of DUKWs — massive amphibious vehicles also known as 'Ducks' — whose commander had omitted to report his location. While out of sight, the platoon was certainly not out of mind and was required urgently for a combined water/land operation.

So at 0700 hours, driving a jeep with several extra jerry cans of petrol, K-rations, water, maps, my service revolver, a rifle and my steel helmet, I set out solo on my unusual mission.

As I crisscrossed the Belgian countryside on a pre-arranged plan, my thoughts were preoccupied with getting the job done and a strong desire to return to Joan and Canada, hopefully in one piece! At the same time, I was being particularly watchful for signs of the enemy who were still in Belgium.

The Belgian people I spoke with, who had endured the harsh Nazi occupation for so long, were very glad to meet a Canadian soldier but were totally unhelpful as far as locating the missing 'Ducks' was concerned.

After a frustrating day of driving around Belgium without the desired result, and with dusk approaching, I decided to settle down for the night at what appeared to be a transit camp recently vacated by the Germans. It was equipped with straw beds known as 'paillasses'. They looked comfortable enough, so I laid down on one and promptly fell asleep for the night. Awakening at first light, I felt very uncomfortable, itching all over, with a pattern of fine red lines etched all over my body. My first thought was that I had contracted some horrible disease. My second thought was that I'd better forget it and get on with the job in hand. Which I did.

The second day of searching was similar to the first, — other than the continued itching — and produced no clue as to the whereabouts of the missing unit. Again, it was getting dark and I had stopped in front of a modest-looking hotel where I decided I could probably get overnight accommodation. I went into the empty lobby and banged on a counter bell. The sound produced a startled proprietor who looked at me in amazement.

"Vous êtes un soldat anglais?" he asked.

"Non et oui — effectivement, je suis un soldat canadien," I replied, French being my second language.

He seemed most perturbed but quickly pulled himself together.

"Quick, put your machine in the coach house," he said in French. "The Germans are still occupying the village and a patrol will be passing here momentarily."

I, of course, complied with alacrity. Together, we covered the jeep with hay, after having first immobilized it by removing the rotor from the distributor cap. This done, we re-entered the hotel via a cellar door just as an enemy patrol marched by the hotel.

It was dark by this time, so the proprietor showed me to a room. He invited me to join him in his quarters for a chat, hot red wine and apples. I accepted and spent an uncomfortable hour with him, restraining myself from scratching and all the while wondering, unnecessarily, if he was in fact an Allied sympathizer and whether or not I would be captured, even worse, by the Germans.

Retiring to my cold damp room and feeling somewhat fearful, I piled every piece of moveable furniture in front of my door — a heavy wardrobe, a table and a couple of chairs. Climbing into bed fully dressed, with revolver and rifle by my side, I tried unsuccessfully to snatch some sleep, the incessant itching keeping me awake. Every so often, I heard the guttural sounds of German voices and listened to steel-shod boots echoing on the cobblestone street in front of the hotel. Finally, around first light, I heard the rumble of heavy vehicles moving, which filled me with hope that the Germans were evacuating the village and retreating. I peeped out a little later and could see no signs of activity. Still later, the proprietor knocked on my door and confirmed that the enemy had in fact departed. Oh, itchy joy unbounded!

I decided I should report back to my headquarters. There, I learned two things. First, the missing unit commander had reported his position, which was well astray of my search. Second, the Headquarters Medical Officer advised that I had not contracted a terrible disease but had acquired some unfriendly lice from the *paillasse* I had slept on the first night. These were quickly dispatched by the simple expedient of sprinkling DDT powder in my winter underwear. What a relief!

In retrospect, all I can say about the whole episode is that I spent one lousy night shivering behind enemy lines!

VE Day in Germany, 1945

by A. John Ellis

The tremendous publicity recently given to V-E Day — May 8th 1945, marking the formal celebration of the Allied victory in Europe during World War II — caused me to look back sixty years to where and what I was doing at that time.

V-E Day, without a doubt, was the most significant day in modern history as it marked the cessation of hostilities in Europe started by the evil madman Adolf Hitler. As a result of his misplaced lust for power, the worldwide estimated combined military and civilian casualties totalled 61,000,000 killed over about a five-year period. This does not include myriad wounded, thought to be in the many millions.

On May 7th, I was a member of the 3rd Canadian Division Headquarters and we were bivouacked on the banks of the Leer River, the border between northern Holland and Germany. The circumstances might be of interest to those who have only a vague idea of the meaning of V-E Day, which was followed shortly thereafter by V-J Day. Those two days marked the return of peace to the world, but only after the wanton slaughter of the aforementioned staggering number of humans.

3rd Canadian Division, on the left flank of the Allied Forces, had been given the task of liberating Holland and had fought the retreating Germans from the south of Holland all the way up to the Leer River. Our affectionate nickname was 'The Water Rats' because we always had the inland seas on our left flank awaiting orders for the next move.

It had been a momentous few days, as history has recorded. On April 29th, Hitler had married Eva Braun in a Berlin bunker and, on the next day, both had committed suicide to avoid capture by Allied troops who were closing in on that shattered city. Hitler's successor, Admiral Karl Dönitz, sent General Alfred Jodl to offer unconditional surrender on May 7th in Reims, France. It was accepted and ceasefire orders were dispatched.

It so happened I was the 3rd Div. Headquarters duty officer that night and received the ceasefire order in the wee hours. A more welcome message is hard to imagine. I kept a copy of it only to have it stolen together with other war trophies back in Canada some years later.

On V-E Day, we were ordered to move to Aurich on the Bremen peninsula and I shall never forget that trip. On a stretch of straight road into Aurich, literally hundreds of fully-armed German troops, looking dispirited and sullen, lined both sides of the road. We were concerned that some hothead would choose to ignore the armistice and start firing at us. Our fears were unfounded and our headquarters group took over an impressive officers' mess in a large military barracks where we spent a couple of days before moving back into Holland. The respite was most welcome after the cool, wet, dangerous, fast-moving and tension-ridden weeks we had experienced before D-Day. From there on, life became less harrowing.

On the first evening in the German Officers' Mess, we decided to have a party for the headquarters officers of our division. The low supply of alcoholic beverages did not hamper our relieved spirits and it was a memorable evening with singing, stories and warrior-dancing around German trophy cups found on the mantelpiece of a huge fireplace. I should add that we filled the cups with petrol and lit them on fire, causing a few pewter cups to melt. There was otherwise no damage, except to the minds of a few German mess stewards who had never before encountered exuberant young Canadian men letting off steam and were no doubt wondering about self-preservation.

The low supply of alcoholic refreshment in our messes became a priority problem. This was solved by a calculated guess that a small German naval installation off the coast probably held the answer to our problem. We had guessed right — two of our officers were dispatched in suitable sea-going vessels, ostensibly to accept the garrison's surrender though that, of course, was a minor consideration. The venture produced an unexpectedly large quantity and variety of beverages.

Utrecht — Holland Right After the War

by A. John Ellis

In late May 1945, I was a GSO3 (Capt.) later to become GSO2 (A/Major) of the 3rd Canadian Division and also President of C Mess. We had ended the war in Aurich, Germany and were sent back to Utrecht, Holland (now The Netherlands) to await transfer to the Japanese theatre or demobilization. En route, we had liberated a very large supply of assorted German booze and, as I recall, our mess had an inventory valued at around $50,000, which we could not possibly consume. The mess only consisted of some twenty officers.

We eventually settled in Utrecht and received a warm welcome from the starving citizens. These people had been very badly treated by the German occupying forces, who stole everything of value, including food. Many of the people were reduced to eating tulip bulbs, which I never tried but was told were scarcely palatable.

We felt very sorry for the plight of the Dutch citizens in Utrecht who had suffered great hardships, particularly in their supply of foodstuffs, which set me to thinking of how we could bring a little cheer into their lives. With this in mind, I decided to arrange a banquet for several hundred citizens using our army kitchens. Consequently, we sent our Camp Commandant and another officer to the Amsterdam black market with a large supply of the liquor we had obtained from the German Navy to exchange for delicacies that we used to create a sumptuous dinner party for a large contingent of the citizenry. We of course enlisted the help of our army cooks and other messes and augmented the delicacies with army rations. The invitation list was compiled with the help of officials of the municipality of Gemeente. We later received a letter of appreciation from a gentleman who had welcomed us to Utrecht and with whom I had struck up a friendship. I believe he was the equivalent of a *burgomeister*.

On another occasion, I organized a 'smoker' for Dutch men at a roadside cafe on the outskirts of Utrecht, using liberated German cigars as well as the liquor. Our guests arrived on bicycles — quite a few of them — all riding on their rims as the Germans had confiscated all bicycle tires for the rubber. Outside the cafe were large concrete anti-tank concrete roadblocks on either side of the road and, while the bicyclists had no trouble arriving at the party on their rims, when it came time to depart after a few unaccustomed drinks, that was another story. Many of our happy participants were now totally incapable of navigating their tire-less machines through the blocks. In the early morning hours, there was quite the crowd of celebrants and bicycles piled up in the ditches on either side of the road. We came to their rescue by organizing a fleet of army jeeps. With difficulty owed to a mixture of alcohol and language issues, we found out where they lived and saw them and their bicycles safely home. Needless to say, a good time was had by all.

While there are many more episodes to relate, I shall close by quoting in part a letter presented to me at the aforementioned banquet by the *Burgomeister* of Utrecht:

> *It is important that you are our host tonight. But it is still more important that you are a soldier of the Canadian Army that gathered so many laurels in this war and have done so much to get us free from the Germans.*
>
> *We, Dutch, owe you very much and, therefore, it is most disagreeable for us that we can't offer you anything because the Germans have stolen nearly all we had.*
>
> *You are a banker, so you are without doubt interested in coinage. Well, the Germans tried to take all our silver and gold coins. But happily, they did not get them all.*
>
> *I offer you hereto a few silver coins of Holland as proof of the great thankfulness the Dutch feel in respect for what the Canadian Army has done for our country.*

While I still have the letter, the coins, done up in an attractive red velvet box, were stolen back in Canada.

Joan on right – paediatric nurse, studying to be
a doctor, at an Alton Hospital in England, 1942.

John, instructor at RMC
Royal Military College,
Kingston Ontario, 1944.

CAPT. and MRS. A. JOHN ELLIS, who were married at Alton, Hampshire, England, on October 6, 1943. Mrs. Ellis was formerly Miss C. Joan Wilson, S.R.N., Capt. Ellis, who went overseas with the Regiment de Maisonneuve in 1940, and has since served as an officer in various establishments on the 1st Canadian Army staff, has been returned to Canada to attend the Army Staff Course at Kingston. Mrs. Ellis, who accompanied him, will remain here, the guest of his parents, Mr. and Mrs. R. L. Ellis, 3434 Northcliffe avenue, Notre Dame de Grace.   Rice Photo

Capt. and Mrs. A. John Ellis, who were married at Alton in Hampshire, England, on October 6th, 1943. Mrs. Ellis was formerly Miss C. Joan Wilson, S.R.N. Capt. Ellis, who went overseas with the Regiment de Maisonneuve in 1940, and has since served as an officer in various establishments on the 1st Canadian Army staff, has been returned to Canada to attend the Army's Staff Course at Kingston. Mrs. Ellis, who accompanied him, will remain here, the guest of his parents, Mr. and Mrs. R. L. Ellis, 3434 Northcliffe avenue, Notre Dame de Grace.

Rice Photo

Ellis, front left, with the officers
of Le Regiment de Maisonneuve
in England, 1940.

Ellis in full battle dress
in Belgium, 1944.

Career Highlights

Interview by Denis Knox

BMO retired senior employee

What do you do when you're 92? Sort of reminds me of the Beatles . . . "Will you still love me when I'm 64?" I asked John Ellis what he does now that he is 92. His response was most interesting. But before I share it with you, let me tell you about this humble man who was, from 1963 to 1971, General Manager of the British Columbia and Yukon Division of BMO. He then became an Executive Vice-President and subsequently was appointed Vice-Chairman and Bank Director. To this day he continues to be an honorary Director of the Bank.

John joined the Bank in Montreal in 1933. Bilingual, he comes from a long line of bankers on both sides of his family. In September 1939, he was called up by the Royal Canadian Air Force for a pilot-officer commission. He actually joined a French-speaking regiment in Montreal and subsequently served in England and

Northwest Europe. He attended a staff training course at the Royal Military College in Kingston in 1943/4 and then returned to Europe as a staff officer where he fought through France, Belgium, Holland and Germany until the ceasefire. In 1945, at the conclusion of his army service, he re-joined the bank.

While in England, he met Joan, whom he married in 1943. Now 64 years later, they both live in a seniors' complex in the Kerrisdale area of Vancouver, called Crofton Manor, which as John describes it, is the "closest thing to paradise".

In 1972, he was elected President of the Canadian Chamber of Commerce. At that time, there were some 750 chambers with over 125,000 members located across Canada. This role was a pivotal one for John in that it permitted him to travel the length and breadth of Canada and also to travel extensively to many international locations. It brought him into contact with political and business leaders from around the world. For John, this represented the pinnacle of his career and he speaks fondly of the opportunity it gave him to positively influence Canadian society.

In the following year, the Canada Development Corporation was created to 'build a better future by developing strong Canadian-controlled and Canadian-managed companies that are important in world markets as well as at home.' John became the first Chairman of the CDC, which had an initial investment of $350 million. He continued in that role for seven years and, when it was eventually wound up, it had investments of over $9 billion and no one had ever lost any money. No doubt his time with the Chamber of Commerce, the CDC and other community interests were some of the reasons why he was awarded the Order of Canada in 1983.

In the late 1950s, John had recognized the rising importance of Japan as an economic and cultural nation. He became involved in the Canada-Japan Society and he and Joan visited that country on many occasions. He was actively involved in the Pacific Basin Economic Council and a senior advisor to a number of Japanese companies. His commitment to the development of Canadian and Japanese relations subsequently lead to his being honoured with the Order of the Rising Sun in 1989 presented by the Emperor of Japan (and duly authorized by Ottawa by way of a special order-in council).

The list of directorships that he has held adds up to over 35, including many corporate entities, universities and not-for-profit organizations. He told me that he finally 'retired' at age 84. I now have a new image of retirement, because for most people, John's definition would translate into a very busy but fulfilling life.

So what does John do now that he is 92? Well, there are 10 grandchildren and 2 great-grandchildren to keep in contact with. There are the 30 to 40 minutes of physical workout in the gym every day (the planned physical activities for the residents of Crofton Manor are not intense enough for him). Twice a month, he attends Laughter Yoga where a good belly-laugh keeps him healthy and young at heart. Every day, he monitors his personal investments and trades his stocks online. He is a prolific writer. Subjects range from ice cream to automobiles to coffee. He is a contributor to the monthly Crofton Manor magazine, *Crofton Manorisms*, doing his research online. Google is his favourite site.

Recently, Simon Fraser University named a room in his honour in the Segal School of Business. John has had a long association with the university. He has funded a number of scholarships in perpetuity for post-graduates in business and commerce. He maintains contact with friends and business associates either by phone or through e-mail. He and his wife entertain family and friends using a private dining room at either Crofton Manor or the Vancouver Club. He tells me that he is blessed with good health and has been lucky.

For me to be able to spend an hour with this giant of a Canadian industry was a humbling experience. Thank you John, for giving me that opportunity.

Denis Knox
at Crofton Manor
November 2007

John was the Chairman of the Corps of Commissioners in Montreal. Here he is in 1960 meeting with members of the Corps.

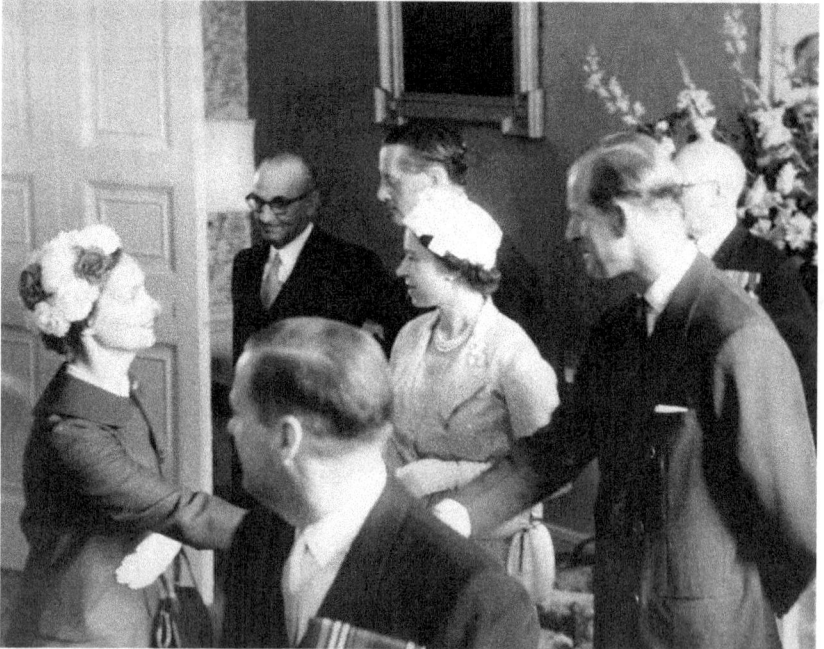

In St. John's, Newfoundland, Queen Elizabeth and Prince Charles are receiving John and Joan Ellis, on the occasion of the cutting of the ribbon for the opening of the Memorial Building Province of Newfoundland, which John was involved in financing, 1961.

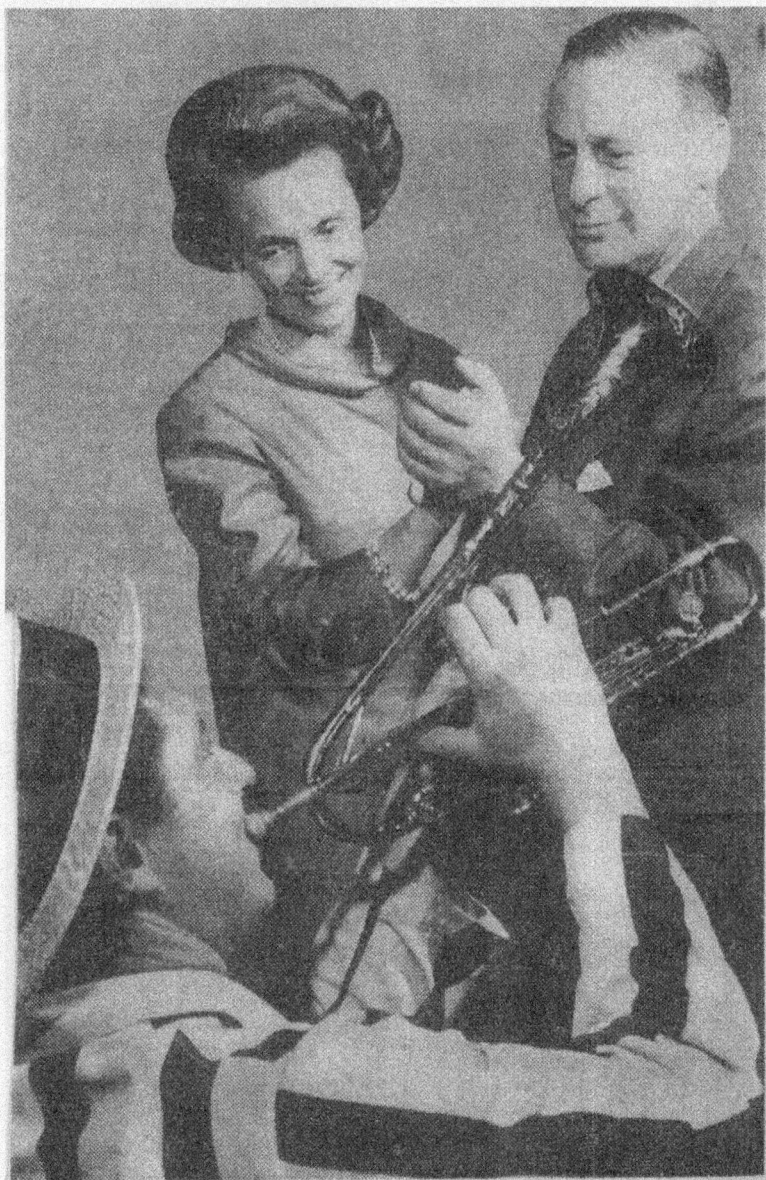

All in a good cause

THE DIXIELAND HORN of Don Clark got Mr. and Mrs. John Ellis dancing at the C.A.R.S. annual cocktail party at the Hotel Vancouver. The rousing event put on by the WA raised money for Rufus Gibbs Lodge of which Mr. Ellis is publicity manager.

Joan and John dancing at the Arthritis Society Annual Cocktail Party in 1964. Joan was a Director of the Society for six years.

Directors Board meeting of the Patagonia Corporation in Tucson, Arizona circa 1967. John is on the right foursome, second from the end.

John used to arrange to fly his directors around the bank branches in the BC interior.

Officiating at the sod turning of the BMO/Bentall Building in downtown Vancouver, 1967. John is third from the right.

Board meeting of Heart and Stroke Foundation in 1971. John was chairman seated at middle of table for three at back of picture.

The BMO building, which was John's headquarters and was subsequently donated to SFU. The University houses its business operations there. John's 100th birthday celebration hosted by SFU was held in this building

John and Joan at Government House in Victoria, 1970 with Dennis and Dorothy Wilson.

John with Pierre Trudeau, Prime Minister of Canada at a meeting as head of the Canadian Chamber of Commerce, 1972.

John with the officers of the Canada Development Corporation of which he was Chairman, 1972.

John delivering a humourous speech in Vancouver, 1972.

Ellis in Ottawa upon being appointed head of the Canadian Chamber of Commerce, 1973.

VANCOUVER

The First Bank Tower is the spectacular, new home of the Bank's main Vancouver branch and of the Divisional Offices for British Columbia.

In a ceremony with Bank chairman, G. Arnold Hart, held on May 27th, The Hon. Walter Owen, Lieutenant-Governor of British Columbia cut the blue ribbon and declared the First Bank Tower open. The branch is fully operational while the divisional offices will be occupied as soon as they are ready.

Attending the ceremonies, held in the open commercial banking area, were some 40 Bank directors, plus members of the Bank executive and numerous other guests. Earlier that afternoon a meeting of the Board was held and then the directors were taken to the First Bank Tower.

Upon arriving at the tower, the directors were escorted on an inspection tour of the new premises by young ladies from the main branch.

Credits

Bank Premises Department: —
R. M. Yeats, MRAIC, ARIBA, Chief Architect

Consultant Architect: —
Frank Musson, MRAIC, ARIBA, Vancouver, B.C.

General Contractor: —
Dominion Construction Co. Ltd.

Tapestries by: —
Joanna Staniszki's, Vancouver, B.C.

† The First Bank Tower is the tallest in Vancouver's new Bentall Centre. Directly in front of the tower is the glass-walled, Personal Banking Pavilion.

The First Bank Tower is the spectacular, new home of the Bank's main Vancouver branch and of the Divisional Offices for British Columbia.

In a ceremony with Bank chairman, G. Arnold Hart, held on May 27th, the Hon. Walter Owen, Lieutenant-Governor of British Columbia cut the blue ribbon and declared the First Bank Tower open. The branch is fully operational while the divisional offices will be occupied as soon as they are ready.

Attending the ceremonies, held in the open commercial banking area, were some 40 Bank directors, plus members of the Bank executives and numerous other guests. Earlier that afternoon a meeting of the Board was held and then the directors were taken to the First Bank Tower.

FIRST BANK TOWER OPENING CEREMONIES

2 Senior vice-president Bob Kayser addresses the guests at the opening ceremonies. Seated behind are (l. to r.): Robert G. Bentall, executive vice-president of Dominion Construction Co. Ltd.; Fred H. McNeil, Bank president; The Hon. Walter Owen, Lieutenant-Governor of British Columbia; Art Phillips, Vancouver Mayor; The Hon. James Sinclair, Bank director; H. Clark Bentall, president of Dominion Construction Co. Ltd.; and A. John Ellis, Bank vice-chairman.

3 Chairman G. Arnold Hart holds the microphone as Lieutenant-Governor, The Hon. Walter Owen cuts the ceremonial ribbon and declares the First Bank Tower open.

Upon arriving at the tower, the directors were escorted on an inspection tour of the new premises by young ladies from the main branch.

1. The First Bank Tower is the tallest in Vancouver's new Bentall Centre. Directly in front of the tower is the glass-walled, Personal Banking Pavilion.

2. Senior vice-president Bob Kayser addresses the guests at the opening ceremonies. Seated behind are (l. to r.): Robert G. Bentall, executive vice-president of Dominion Construction Co. Ltd.; Fred H. McNeil, Bank president; The Hon. Walter Owen, Lieutenant- Governor of British Columbia; Art Phillips, Vancouver Mayor; The Hon. James Sinclair, Bank director; H. Clark Bentall, president of Dominion Construction Co. Ltd.; and A. John Ellis, Bank vice-chairman.

The First Canadian Bank

Bank of Montreal

University Campus
P.O. Box 160
Fredericton, N.B.
E3B 4Z1

Telephone No.

April 27, 1976

Mr. A. John Ellis
c/o Bank of Montreal
Main Office
Vancouver, B. C.

Dear Mr. Ellis:

I was most interested to read of your recent retirement as
Chairman of the Board in Vancouver and I am writing to offer my
warmest wishes for good health and much happiness for the future.
I am delighted that you will continue as a Director since I feel
you will always make a major contribution as a member of that
Board.

I have always been most grateful for the important part you
played in my appointment at the Campus Branch. With the busy
years that have intervened, you may have long forgotten that it
was the great support which you gave to the idea of a "lady
manager" that finally brought the decision in my favour. It has
been gratifying to watch the progress of other women in the Bank
and I feel that a great debt is owed to you yourself and others
who had the courage to promote the first manager of the distaff
side.

I recall with great pleasure the luncheon which you had for
my two friends, Pat Morrison and Geth Coolen, and myself on my
first trip west to Vancouver in 1965. I was delighted to see you
again and have thought of you on many occasions since that time.
I had my second trip west only last summer but just to Calgary an
Edmonton. I hope one day to get back to Vancouver again.

You may be interested to know that our staff which numbered
four in 1963 is now up to 32. I recently had an increase of
Branch Grade here to 9 which is gratifying. It is a busy spot

but I am fortunate indeed in having an excellent staff which makes my job a much easier one than it would otherwise be.

Again, Mr. Ellis, my warmest wishes for much happiness in the future and with kindest personal regards to Mrs. Ellis and yourself.

Very sincerely,

Becky Watson

Miss R. E. Watson
Manager

REW/rjh

Copy of a letter from Miss R. E. Watson, manager of the University Campus Branch in Fredericton, to John Ellis upon his retirement. Ms. Watson was the first woman in the bank's history to become a branch manager in 1963. John had instigated her appointment — the beginning of many female executive appointments in the bank.

Joan and John in Japan, 1983.

John receiving the Order of Canada from the Governor General of Canada Edward Schreyer, 1983.

Ribbon cutting event in 1992 to mark the opening of the magnificent new Canadian Embassy in Tokyo, Japan. John and Joan attended and arranged for several prominent Japanese and their wives to attend with them, followed by a banquet dinner party. The Prime Minister is third from the right.

Joan and John on the occasion where he received the Order of Canada in Ottawa, 1983.

Ellis shaking hands with Prime Minister Brian Mulrooney in Ottawa.

Chris Shannon, Headmaster of Lower Canada College, with Robert Ellis on his right and John on his left.

The Family in Photos

Joan Wilson at age 2.

Elizabeth in front of Robert, Joan and Susan in Halifax, 1952.

Left to right on floor: Elizabeth, Susan, cousin Kitty and Robert.

Same group at Halifax, 1955 with the rest of the family and relatives.

Joan at Halifax, 1953.

Elizabeth on her graduation from UBC, 1968.

Joan playing a 30-pound salmon that she happily boated. John is on the right. They were guests of the late Frank Griffiths in 1966.

John, Joan, Lisa, Stephanie, Susan, Jennifer, and Severin. Vancouver, 1983.

Rob and Gwen Ellis. Vancouver, 1985.

Ellis home at 3851 Marguerite Street in Vancouver.

Jacqui and Scott Ellis with their three children in Kamloops, BC in 2016.

Stephanie, John, Lisa, Joan, Gwen with young Scott, Robert, Jennifer, Susan, Andrea with son David, 1986.

One of Joan's paintings in oil. She was highly talented and sold many pictures.

An abstract inspired by nature.

Sugaring off in Quebec.

She even painted me.

The Ellis Clan at John's 100th birthday party hosted by SFU.

Letters from Crofton Manor

Humour

by A. John Ellis

A few years ago, a group of wordsmiths were searching for the best humour story ever told. They came up with the following. You be the judge:

> Sherlock Holmes and his faithful companion, Dr. Watson, were on a camping trip. After a good meal and a bottle of wine, they crawled into their tent and were soon fast asleep. Some hours later, Holmes wakes up and nudges his friend awake.
>
> "Watson, look up at the sky and tell me what you see."
>
> "I see millions and millions of stars, Holmes," Watson replied.
>
> "And what do you deduce from that?"
>
> Watson ponders a minute.

"Well, astronomically, it tells me that there are millions of galaxies and potentially billions of planets.

Astrologically, I observe that Saturn is in Leo.

Homologically, I deduce the time is approximately a quarter past three.

Meteorologically, I suspect that we will have a beautiful day.

Theologically, I can see that God is all–powerful, and that we are a small and insignificant part of the universe.

What does it tell you Holmes?"

Holmes is silent for a moment then...

"Watson, you idiot," he said. "Someone has stolen our tent!"

Join the Humour and Laughter Gang

by A. John Ellis

Some people contend that improving lifestyle and stretching longevity is no laughing matter. Wrong! The more you laugh the happier you'll feel, and the happier you feel, the longer you will probably live. A sort of *quod erat demonstrandum* situation. If, however, you depart prematurely, come back and I'll debate it with you.

Here at Crofton Manor, there are monthly Laughter Yoga sessions and, so far, nobody attending has shown any sign of deterioration! Most, if not all participants, have fun and go away feeling uplifted. Anyone capable of eating unassisted and who is mobile, with or without a walker or cane, should give it a whirl. Age is no barrier. Personally, I find it easier than ever to laugh at all human foibles, particularly my own!

Anyhow, as I no longer have been required to make any momentous decisions in recent years (such as, should

I try to prevent anyone from putting overalls in Mrs. Murphy's chowder?), I decided to research humour and laughter and what I found follows. Incidentally, I think the soups and chowders here are the absolute best even without the inclusion of overalls.

Humour and laughter go hand-in-hand, so I make no apology for mixing the two in this ramble. Webster's *New Twentieth Century Dictionary Unabridged* describes laughter as:

> Laughter. An expression of mirth, manifested in certain convulsive and partly involuntary actions of the muscles of respiration, by means of which air, being expelled from the chest in a series of 'jerks', produces a succession of short abrupt sounds, certain movements of the muscles of the face, and often other parts of the body also taking place; also any expression of merriment, derision etc., perceivable in the countenance, as in the eyes. Syn. Merriment, glee, ridicule, cachinnation, contempt.

Dr. Webster excelled himself, don't you think? I stumbled over the word 'cachinnation'. I bet you will too — it means to laugh loudly, noisily with mirthless laughter. Aren't you glad you've read so far, as I suspect most of you have learned a new word? But watch it, folks, if you show signs of cachinnation!

The elaborate explanation of 'laughter' reminds me of the old saying: "Cast your bread upon the waters and it will come back in the form of a roast beef sandwich."

So, I decided the simpler school dictionary definition of humour is more acceptable. It states:

Humour
1. A state of mind; mood as, he is in a bad humour
2. The capacity to see or appreciate things that are funny; as, a sense of humour
3. The quality of being funny or amusing, as, the humour of a story

It seems apparent Webster believed laughter applied only to the human species and one must agree. To begin with, invertebrates should be ruled out. Have you ever heard a worm laugh or thought you detected in him/her a sense of humour? Come to think of it, all worms I have met have had little to be happy about, especially when being impaled on a hook for the purpose of catching an unwary fish destined for a frying pan! In different ways, the same applies to all invertebrates.

So, let's look at non-human vertebrates. Dachshunds, dolphins, monkeys, parrots and some other birds appear, superficially at least, to show signs of humourous dispositions. You may have observed monkeys at a zoo playing tricks on each other (along with other unmentionable habits!) Dolphins squeal in apparent delight when tickled and some dachshunds I have known affect their versions of human smiles when greeting their favourite two-legged friends. Without a doubt, there are other animals with similar characteristics, but it seems safe to contend that only the human race has laughter built into its psyche. The *Encyclopaedia Britannica* states that laughter is a human phenomenon, and among lower animals a very rare occurrence, if indeed it exists at all. So humans can be said to be the laughing beings *par excellence*.

Most people love to laugh whenever appropriate such as a "hail fellow, well met" type of approach to most situations. The therapeutic value of laughter has been recognized for centuries. In the Bible, Proverbs 17:22 says, "A merry heart doeth good like a medicine, but a broken spirit drieth the bones." Lord Byron said, "Always laugh when you can, it is cheap medicine." An anonymous quote: "Laughter and humour can help make the unbearable a little more bearable."

A book could be written about humour, laughter and what makes us laugh. We all have differing motivations and each of us is pretty much aware of why we laugh. Some of us particularly enjoy a gentle *ha-ha-ha* type of laughter, while others prefer the *ho-ho-ho* form, commonly known as a good belly laugh. Some enjoy having a strong sense of the ridiculous, which causes them much merriment, while others get a real laugh from slapstick comedy. Still others specialize in self-deprecating humour, which is generally the most acceptable type of personal humour. The worst type of so-called humour is trying to get a laugh at the expense of an often defenceless third party. The perpetrator is usually an insecure person to be pitied. Many of us enjoy an author who has a subtle approach to life's foibles. The late PG Wodehouse was a master of this, and has given countless readers a lot of laughs over his light-hearted and amusing anecdotes. Lucky is the person who can extract humour and the ability to laugh even when the going is tough.

Group laughter can be contagious when large numbers of people are gathered to watch and listen to a comedy or a comedian. The humour may not be great, but laughter spreads like wildfire when an audience is looking to be amused. Incidentally, when the comedian or comedy has been successful in getting laughs, most people go away feeling pleased and happy.

Unanticipated comedy occurs frequently, catches us by surprise and makes us burst out laughing. The responses given by six-year-old students bears testimony to this and may provide a few chuckles as a fitting conclusion to this article. Their teacher had collected well-known proverbs. She gave each child in her class the first half of a proverb with the second half to be filled in by the student. Some of the answers are hilarious:

1. Better to be safe than ... to punch a 5th grader
2. Strike while the ... bug is close
3. It's always darkest before ... Daylight Savings Time
4. Never underestimate the power of ... termites
5. Don't bite the hand that ... looks dirty
6. No news is ... impossible
7. A miss is as good as ... a mister
8. You can't teach an old dog new ... math
9. If you lie down with dogs, you'll ... stink in the morning
10. Love all, trust ... me
11. The pen is mightier than the ... pigs
12. An idle mind is ... the best way to relax
13. Where there's smoke there's ... pollution
14. Happy the bride who ... gets all the presents
15. A penny saved is ... not much

16. Two's company, three's ... the Musketeers
17. Laugh and the world laughs with you, cry and you ... have to blow your nose
18. There are none so blind as ... Stevie Wonder
19. Children should be seen and not ... spanked or grounded
20. If at first you don't succeed ... get new batteries
21. When the blind leadeth the blind ... get out of the way
22. Better late than ... pregnant

I always get a few *ho-ho-hos* from the wisdom of these first graders, and feel much better after I dry my eyes and blow my nose!

Conversation & Laughter

by A. John Ellis

When things look grim and one starts to take life too seriously, it is obviously time to relax and look at other sides of life — if you can. Personally, at such times, I find refuge in a lot of semi-ridiculous nonsense. Such as "depression is merely anger without enthusiasm", as Steven Wright contends, along with gems like "the early bird may get the worm, but the second mouse gets the cheese!" Think about the logic of that one for a while and you'll be forced to agree, provided there was a cheese-baited mousetrap.

Scientifically-minded people like to ponder both light and heavy subjects. For instance, the speed of light, which they delight in telling you equals 299,792,458 metres per second or 186,000 miles per second. Ask them then: what is the speed of dark? Following this, ask for a definition of light and dark bearing in mind that light contains no dark, and dark has no light — so what's what? You could be in for hours of entertaining conversation if your informant is a true scientist and a disciple of Albert Einstein. You'll soon forget all about your troubles if you can get a conversation going along these lines.

There are myriad conversation starters, some of them mind-boggling and some simplicity personified. Some are simple statements of fact, some fiction and a lot of them concern subjects many people have either never thought about or never known about, but all are pretty well guaranteed to elicit some comments.

If you have an appreciation of things ridiculous and/or trivial then read on; otherwise put down this light-hearted article and retreat into more erudite areas or even dullsville — if you must. However, if looking for conversation starters, have a gander at the following short list of sense and nonsense, some of it true and some false.

- A cat has 32 muscles controlling each ear.
- A dragonfly has a lifespan of 6 months.
- A goldfish has a memory span of three seconds.
- Almonds are members of the peach family.
- A 'jiffy' is an actual unit of time for 1/1000th of a second.
- Babies are born without true kneecaps.
- In your lifetime, you will spend 6 months waiting at red lights.
- Women blink nearly twice as much as men.
- There are more chickens than people in the world.
- The winter of 1932 was so cold that Niagara Falls froze completely solid

So, next time you're sitting with one or more people staring into space and exchanging only occasional grunts, try quoting one of the ten statements listed before and see what happens. Take the goldfish statement of having an ultra short memory span for instance. This recently led to a half-hour discussion covering the birds, bees, animals and humans suffering from dementia and why.

A lot of people enjoy the distraction of humour, of which there is lots everywhere, depending on how you look at it. You may think that an apple a day keeps the doctor away — there is probably some truth in it but one thing for sure is that a laugh a day helps to do the same thing. Laughing has even greater ramifications as scientists have estimated that laughing a hundred times equals the same physical exertion as a ten-minute workout on a rowing machine or fifteen minutes on a stationary exercise bicycle. How about that! And did you realize that laughing works out the diaphragm, abdominal, respiratory, facial, leg and back muscles? A pioneer in laughter research, William Fry, reported it took ten minutes on a rowing machine for his heart rate to reach the level it would after just one minute of hearty laughter.

Laughter is a natural stress-buster, which makes us feel happy and more tolerant of those around us. It is almost a truism that regular laughter sessions will improve health and promote a feeling of well-being in most people. It is a gentle exercise available and recommended for practically everyone, and especially recommended for people who are sedentary. By reducing our stress, blood pressure is reduced, depression is less oppressive and our immune systems are enhanced. Seemingly humdrum lives become far more meaningful and quality of life dramatically improves. Anecdotal evidence abounds about miraculous cures in otherwise hopeless cases who have undergone laughter therapy.

In recent years, there has been an accelerating realization that laughter is a marvellous therapeutic pathway to better health for many people. So much so that laughter clubs have sprung up all around the world and there are said to be five thousand of them in more than fifty countries. There is a laughter club here in Vancouver, which the writer has not had time to research, though is planning to do so shortly.

You won't finish this article without a laugh. You may be interested in a couple of stories:

First, a man and his friend were playing golf at the local club. One of the guys is about to chip onto the green when he sees a long funeral procession on the road next to the course. He stops in mid-swing, takes off his cap, closes his eyes and kneels down in prayer. Afterwards, his friend says, "Wow, that is the most thoughtful and touching thing I have ever witnessed. You are truly a kind man." His friend replies, "Yeah, well, we were married for thirty-five years."

Second, two men were sitting at a bar and drinking rather heavily. After a while, they became unruly and started trading personal insults. Finally, the older of the two blurted out, "You're not going to like this, but I'm telling you now that I've slept with your mother." The younger man paid no attention to the disclosure, which very much annoyed the drinking partner who yelled out again very loudly, "I've slept with your mother." By this time, the whole establishment and guests were listening intently to the exchanged barbs and waiting for the response to this last insult. The younger man didn't turn a hair and quietly said, "I think we should go home now, Dad. You're drunk!"

Hopefully, you got a couple of laughs from the foregoing and feel better already. Actually humourous stories are not necessary to induce laughter, as the students of the laugh clubs will tell you, but for demonstration purposes in a written article, they help.

Ain't We Got Fun

by A. John Ellis

Some of us recall the 1921 song "Ain't We Got Fun", which was popular for many years. Some of us remember parts of the chorus, which included these couplets:

> Ev'ry morning, ev'ry evening
> Ain't we got fun?
>
> In the winter, in the summer
> Don't we have fun?
>
> In the meantime, in between time
> Ain't we got fun?

The song lyrics were built around a lot of situations and designed to point out the merits of having fun no matter what. It's a fitting introduction to the really fun Laughter Yoga sessions I introduced to Crofton Manor.

Laughter Yoga is the brainchild of a Dr. Madan Kataria, who created it some eleven years ago. Today, countless people all over the world enjoy the benefits of a daily dose of laughter at laughter clubs or their workplaces. It has spread to some fifty countries and it is estimated there are five thousand active clubs worldwide.

Most of us have, on occasion, grudgingly accepted invitations to parties, which we anticipated would be colossally boring, but we ended up having a marvellous time. This, to some extent, is happening at the Laughter Yoga sessions and anyone passing up the opportunity to attend is missing a real treat. There are many reasons for not attending — including scepticism, shyness, undue self-consciousness and other personal governors — but for most, all reservations will be swept aside by an initial session. Give it a whirl and the chances of being disappointed are likely to be close to nil.

We are born with the gift of laughter, but we learn to be serious. Do you know that it is estimated that children laugh 150 to 300 times daily whereas adults on average laugh only 10 to 12 times daily? Many of us are aware that laughter makes us feel well. Regular laughter can have a profound impact on our health and well-being. Laughter is gentle exercise that fills our lungs with oxygen, clears our breathing passages and releases a mixture of chemicals and hormones in our bodies. It is a known stress-buster, lowering blood pressure, lifting depression and generally boosting immune systems.

You too can keep healthier by regular bouts of laughter. We at Crofton Manor had an opportunity to test that assertion. First, residents had a sample of it at a recent Wellness Fair when a large group, many openly sceptical about the exercise, found themselves in due course practically rolling on the floor from uninhibited and genuine laughter. We then had another, ongoing opportunity when professionally-led Laughter Yoga classes started in May that year.

There are, no doubt, some people who consider the exercises somewhat childish, but they are missing the focal points of the mental stimulation and health, which laughter induces. Most who attend a session end up feeling mentally and physically better. I can testify to that.

Come on and let that child lurking within you hear the light of day at a Laughter Yoga session, maybe even here at Crofton Manor. We are fortunate to have astute management with a pioneering perspective offering all residents a unique opportunity to feel better. So attend the classes — with your family members if you wish. Add a touch of happiness to your life!

Writing & the Writer's Club

by A. John Ellis

Most educated adults, at one time or another, have harboured a desire to go into print by way of an autobiography or short stories covering certain episodes in their lives t they consider to be of interest to others. These feelings are usually engendered by a wish to inform their families and relatives of their background and accomplishments, which would otherwise be lost to posterity. Some even feel they may have a book or more to write.

Many of the would-be writers find it difficult to get started and the following ideas may be helpful to them.

The distinguished author, historian, teacher and award winner, Charlotte Gray, said that history is not just about yesterdays or dead people — it is a fluid continuum and we are part of it. She loves bringing history to life and giving her readers an intimate journey into a past that's full of drama, larger-than-life personalities and links to the present. In our vibrant collective memory, she says we have enough fascinating stories and lessons learned to fill volumes. Her works and viewpoints are inspiring to say the least. She originally started just as the rest of us must do, although few can emulate her successes in word power.

Speaking of word power, Rudyard Kipling contended that words are the most powerful drugs used by mankind. Mark Twain advised that if you are tempted to write, you should get facts first, then you can distort them as much as you please! For anyone thinking of writing but doesn't know how to start, those two ideas should be incentive enough when coupled with the thought that writing is an exploration. You start from nothing and learn as you go. Another notable drew the simile of an automobile travelling in a heavy fog when the headlights provided illumination for a few yards only, but with careful driving, the planned trip could be made if very slowly. So too the beginner writer, carefully and slowly plodding along sentence by sentence and keeping Mark Twain's humourous advice in mind, ends up producing a readable story. Of course, there are exceptions in writers who rattle off acceptable prose at a great rate. You may be one or the other or somewhere in-between. In any event, why not give writing a whirl, even if you have only the slightest urge?

There are significant moments in everyone's life that can be recorded. Why not write about them for starters? It can be great fun.

I've Got a Feeling I'm Falling

by A. John Ellis

Quite a few of you readers will remember the popular music composition of the Roaring Twenties, which shares its title with that of this short article. The lyrics were composed by the legendary 'Fats' Waller and the song was, of course, a romantic, sentimental tune on the lips of many flappers and their boyfriends of the day. Or should that be night?

The twenties were, of course, some ninety years ago, but a lot of us who still remember those days have the feeling we may now be exposed to falling quite literally. Some are taking action to avoid falls while others are just trusting in luck. The incidence of seniors experiencing falls causing serious injuries, sometimes even resulting in death, is on the rise, at least in North America. Try to avoid being one of them. Just relying on canes, walkers and motorized buggies is not enough.

If you can possibly do it — with your doctors' agreement if necessary — you should exercise daily and take advantage of the sessions being offered here at Crofton Manor six days a week. You can participate as little or as fully as you wish, either sitting or standing. Go at your own pace. Regular attendance will help keep your muscles and bones in shape and it's almost a given that you will feel more cheerful.

All courses offered here at Crofton will help improve your physique and probably your outlook on life in general. So why not try them all? The only things you have to lose are pain and depression!

How About Tea

by A. John Ellis

Even though tea can hardly be considered a glamorous substance, it has been the cause of much excitement, as well as being the beverage of choice for billions of the world's population. There is a wealth of interesting information about tea, so it is interesting to consider some of the history and the whys and wherefores of this staple.

It is not unreasonable to believe that tea shrubs started to grow on this planet following the retreat of the last major ice age thousands of years ago, but it wasn't until 2737 B.C. that tea leaves were first used to brew a beverage. Legend has it that Emperor Shennong of China, famed for tasting hundreds of herbs to determine their value as medicine, had at the time required all drinking water to be boiled for hygienic purposes. When on a visit in the countryside, his entourage stopped for rest and refreshment. The servants began to boil water when burning leaves from a bush fell into the boiling water, creating a brown liquid. The emperor decided to taste the liquid and found it potable and pleasant — the drink of tea had been discovered!

Generations after generations have been brewing it happily ever since. That means that our populations of tea drinkers have been appreciating tea for almost five thousand years. Present-day purveyors of fried chicken, hamburgers, coffee, liquors and whatnot can never hope to challenge such a record.

There are three main types of tea.

Black tea has been fully oxidized or fermented and yields a hearty-flavoured amber brew. Green tea, which is not oxidized, has a more delicate taste than black tea and is becoming popular because it is said to have medicinal properties such as reducing cancer risk. Oolong tea, used mainly in China, is partly oxidized.

It is interesting to trace chronologically the spread of tea's popularity. China was the first to embrace it, followed by Japan, India, Europe, America and finally, England. Many believe that England was the originator of tea-drinking culture, but surprisingly the first samples of tea reached England between 1652 AD and 1654 AD, well behind the pack! It is recorded that tea-mania swept across England, as it had earlier spread throughout Holland and France. Tea importation in England rose from 40,000 pounds in 1699 to an annual average of 240,000 pounds by 1708.

Concentrating on England, it should be noted that the English developed the concept of 'tea gardens', following the example of Dutch 'tavern garden teas'. At English tea gardens, ladies and gentlemen took their tea out-of-doors, where diversions were offered by way of orchestras, concerts, gambling and other distractions such as fireworks at night. It is reported that it was at just such a tea garden that Lord Nelson — who masterminded the defeat of Napoleon at sea — met the great love of his life, Emma, later Lady Hamilton. Women were permitted to enter a mixed public gathering for the first time without social criticism. As the gardens were public, British society mixed freely there for the first time, cutting across lines of class and birth.

The age-old tradition of pouring the milk into the cup before pouring the tea originated in England and the explanation is both simple and practical. Delicate china cups may crack when very hot tea is poured into them, hence it was thought advisable to pour the cold milk in first.

The subject of tea conjures up gentle, happy times. Still, while for the most part this is a truism, the desire to acquire this universally-admired commodity has been the cause of tremendous violence in the past. A prime example of this was the Opium Wars of the nineteenth century, which broke out with the English using force with China for so-called free trade — *i.e.*, the right to sell opium in exchange for tea. By 1842, England had gained enough military advantage to enable it to sell opium in China undisturbed until 1908. The English tea monopoly was finally broken when America entered the tea trade, paying for tea with gold rather than opium and using faster ships that reached the markets well ahead of their competitors. China has never forgiven the English for introducing heroin to their country.

It was during the nineteenth century that the excitement caused by tea peaked. Those were the days of the magnificent clipper sailing ships, whose captains vied with each other in the rush to get tea to markets. The most prominent of those beautiful clippers were the *Cutty Sark* and the *Thermopylae*. The latter was sold in 1895 to the Portuguese and deliberately torpedoed in 1906 during target practice by the Portuguese navy. The *Cutty Sark* suffered a kinder fate, having been sold in 1922 to the Cornish Captain Dowman, who began restoring her to her former glory. In time, she became a naval training vessel. In 1954, *Cutty Sark* made her final journey home to dry dock in Greenwich, London. She became a popular tourist attraction, protected by the Cutty Sark Trust, and is the last remaining example of the great clippers.

Jumping ahead to the devastating air raids on England during WWII, after the heavy stresses of the day, the people's philosophy was "Oh well, let's put on the kettle and have a cup of tea." When supplies of tea were short, the saying shifted to "Let's put on the kettle and have a nice cup of hot water!" Undoubtedly, tea — and even hot water — has a soothing effect.

During WWII, at least one of the major London hotels held 'tea dances' for officers of the Armed Forces on Saturday afternoons. These were thoroughly enjoyable events during tense times and greatly appreciated by the participants, myself included.

Tea dances in present times seem almost universally to be coming back into vogue. For example, "Tea and Trumpets" in Vancouver is proving to be highly popular.

At my home in Crofton Manor, the Thursday afternoon tea fixture is one of the highlights of each week, well attended by both residents and their guests.

In the USA, tea is more popular than ever. There is a reawakening of interest in tea as many citizens seek a more positive, healthier lifestyle. As has been done for many years at the Empress Hotel in Victoria BC, fine hotels throughout the United States are re-establishing or planning afternoon tea services for the first time.

Tea drinking in China, which had suffered doctrinal rejection during the first decades of Communism, along with many other traditional features of the country, is now making a strong comeback. A recent newspaper article by Martin Fackler reports that a Disney-like amusement park, dedicated entirely to tea, has been established in the region that grows China's famous oolong tea. Although hours from the nearest airport, it is attracting thousands of Chinese tourists. Rising wealth in the PRC has brought a newfound sense of self-confidence and, as a consequence, many new tea shops throughout the country are being opened and drawing crowds both young and old.

Today, tea of all types is being recommended for health reasons. Rosie Schwartz, a Toronto-based consulting dietician as well as an author on diet who recently published an article entitled "A Porcelain Cup of Power" in the *National Post*, notes that beyond its already-known health benefits, tea now is being recognized as an effective deterrent against many diseases. In part, she says that while a cup of tea may seem as simple as a beverage can be, it's actually a complex brew of potential disease fighters. Among the compounds it contains are polyphenols, kissing cousins to the protective substances identified in red wine, chocolate and a variety of fruit and vegetables. One tip she offers is that a quick dip of the tea bag in hot water won't yield maximum polyphenol levels. Instead, she says, aim for a steep of at least three or four minutes. The list of potential benefits of tea seems to be growing in leaps and bounds, she adds. Scientists have linked tea consumption to protection against common ills such as cardiovascular disease, certain cancers, high blood pressure and Alzheimer's disease. Her list of the benefits of tea-drinking goes on and on, but space does not permit further elaboration. Suffice to say that tea is increasing greatly in popularity, is a healthy antioxidant beverage, particularly green tea, and is here to stay. Many people are seeking relaxation and contentment. Leisurely tea consumption, either solo or in a party, may hold some of the answers. So if you're not already an advocate — jump on the tea-wagon and enjoy!

And Now About Coffee

by A. John Ellis

Asked what the companion word to 'tea' is, the average person is likely to respond 'coffee'. How fitting it is that the two beverages are linked in our minds. Both were discovered in most interesting and accidental ways. Tea, some five thousand years ago, by tea shrub leaves falling by chance into boiling water and creating a pleasant, potable drink that has increased in popularity ever since. Coffee came later, but still many centuries ago, when legend has it that an Ethiopian goat herder witnessed his charges become skittish, frisky and frolicsome after eating berries from shrubs, which, of course, were coffee plants. Being of an inquiring mind and with nothing better to do, he tried chewing a few of the red berries himself and, lo and behold, he began to feel like we all do today after drinking a coffee — receiving that jolt — which has become an important part of millions of people's lives worldwide. In fact, coffee has surpassed tea as the hot beverage of choice and it is safe to say is universally the most popular drink with an estimated 500 billion cups consumed annually.

Like teahouses, coffeehouses were established in England where they became known as 'penny universities', as a penny was charged for entrance and a cup of coffee. In due course, one of these houses, Lloyd's Coffee House, evolved into the giant insurance company Lloyd's of London. Similar coffeehouses opened under different names in many other countries over the years and obviously became highly popular. In recent years here in North America, we have witnessed the establishment of coffee purveyors such as Starbucks and seen them grow at a very rapid rate, although the penny cup has of course grown to several dollars, with elaborate concoctions and flavours on offer and finding ready acceptance.

As a matter of special interest to us Crofton Manor residents, the name 'kaffeeklatsch' was coined in Germany early in the twentieth century when people met for afternoon coffee. The term was a derogatory one, implying women's gossip at the affairs. However, the interpretation is now much kinder with the implication being merely good conversation over an enlivening cup of coffee.

While drinking coffee in moderation is said to be harmless, like many other enjoyable things, we are told excessive consumption could be injurious to our constitutions. So much so that certain segments of our worldwide community, such as the Mormons, prohibit the consumption of coffee. Some Christians considered coffee to be the devil's drink. One of the early popes was advised of this, but after trying it for himself, found it so pleasant a drink that instead of banishing it, he 'baptized' it, declaring that it would be a sin to leave the infidels of the Ottoman Empire with the exclusive enjoyment of such a superior beverage.

There is a wealth of information on the subject of coffee with tidbits such as the legend that the first coffee shop was opened in Turkey in the fifteenth century by Ottomans. It became so popular and addictive that legislation was created allowing a wife to divorce her husband if he failed to give her a daily ration of coffee!

Espresso machines, cappuccino, percolators, drip coffeemakers, one-cup coffee makers, mug warmers, instant coffee, decaffeinated coffee, new ways of cultivation and other refinements have kept appearing over the years along with special roasting techniques to a point where there would appear to be very little new to be discovered or invented in the coffee world.

As an aside, old-timers will probably recall the oblique reference to coffee in the popular pre–WWII song, which indicated that it had become a regular fixture in our daily lives. The songsters of the day were belting out the refrain:

> You're the cream in my coffee,
> You're the salt in my stew,
> You will always be
> My necessity,
> I can't do without you.

Weight-watchers today would be horrified by the implied routine use of cream and salt, but back then people were not really weight-conscious.

In closing, if you happen to observe any Crofton Manor residents acting like the legendary goat herder's charges, blame it on our delightful kaffeeklatsch, which is in operation seven days a week in the Oak Lounge. It is well-stocked with juices, buns and tea of your choosing, but most importantly: coffee. If you haven't done so, join in the fun and, if you wish, become "skittish, frisky and frolicsome"!

How About Water

by A. John Ellis

Whether soporifically soaking in a warm bath, shivering in a shower or drinking a glass of clear water, have you ever stopped to wonder about water itself? What is it, where did it come from, what are its properties, how much of it is there, what are its future prospects and so on? Through my layman and non-professional point of view, I will examine some factors of possible interest.

For starters, you might like to have a crack at answering the following true-or-false quiz:

1. Water contracts when it freezes.
2. Water has a high surface tension.
3. Condensation is water coming out of air.
4. More things can be dissolved in sulphuric acid than in water.
5. Rainwater is the purest form of water.
6. Raindrops are tear-shaped.

7. Water boils quicker at the top of Grouse Mountain than at Jericho Beach.
8. There is more water drunk at Crofton Manor than alcohol.
9. The dog population here would like to paddle in muddy waters if given half a chance.

(Answers at the end)

Our total water supply is always moving around in a liquid state, as a vapour or in the form of ice. The Earth is a sort of a closed circuit when it comes to water and the total volume of water has changed little since the beginning of time. It is quite conceivable that the water you are drinking today was once filling one of Caesar's Roman baths. ("Aha!" you say. "That probably accounts for the special bouquet I noticed in the drinking water last week!") The same old water is continually being recycled all around our universe.

The US Geological Survey says there is a theory that much of Earth's water came from comets hitting the planet billions of years ago. Where the balance came from, God only knows and She won't tell. Ah, sweet mystery of life, there are so many unexplained questions and this is one of them!

You or any other living creature couldn't exist without water. About 60% of our bodies is comprised of water, the brain is made up of 70% water, (the older I get, the more I think mine has about 25% cornmeal mush), the lungs approximately 90% and our blood 82%. Some alcoholics contend that their blood is mainly alcohol, which acts as an anti-freeze but don't you believe them

— their blood is still about 82% water and falling asleep in a snow bank is a no-no!

Most people know that chemical description of water is H2O and let it go at that, possibly not fully appreciating it means one atom of oxygen is bound to two atoms of hydrogen. The hydrogen atoms are 'attached' to one side of the oxygen atom, resulting in a water molecule having a positive charge on the side where the hydrogen atoms are and a negative charge on the other side, where the oxygen atom is. Since opposite electrical charges attract, water molecules tend to attract each other making water kind of 'sticky'.

Water is called the 'universal solvent' because it dissolves more substances than any other liquid. This means that wherever water goes, either through the ground or through our bodies, it takes along valuable chemicals, minerals and nutrients. Pure water is colourless and has no taste or odour. It has a neutral pH of 7.

The world has a total water volume of 333,000,000 cubic miles, but surface water sources constitute only about 300 cubic miles representing about 1/10,000% of the total, yet rivers are the source of most of the water we use at present. It is highly likely that, in due course, science will produce ways to economically utilize the presently non-potable waters. Oceans hold 97.24% of the world's total water volume.

On the raindrop shape question, there is this to say. When a drop of water comes out of a faucet, it has a tear shape. That is because the back end of the water drop sticks to the water still in the tap until it can't hold on any longer. A raindrop however, looks more like a small bun as gravity and surface tension take effect. As rain falls, the air below the drop pushes up from the bottom, causing the drop to flatten out a bit. The strong surface tension of water holds a drop together, resulting in a bun shape (but without the raisins or sesame seeds!).

Water provides humans with a wonderful medium for relaxation and exercise, but if you can't swim, stay away from it. You may have heard of the non-swimmer atheist who had fallen overboard from a cruise vessel. He was going down for the proverbial third time and was heard to shout out, "Oh my God, if there is a God, save my soul if I have a soul."

Having read the foregoing, your reaction is probably "So what?" My reaction is that all this and fifty cents buys you a bad cigar and nobody forced you to read it anyway!

Quiz answers:

1. False
2. True
3. True
4. False
5. False
6. False
7. True
8. Ask Mr. Andy Cook
9. True (we checked with the dogs)

Life's Vital Substance

by A. John Ellis

In our Western world, we are inclined to take potable water for granted. Generally speaking, it's only when we are faced with a polluted supply that we realize how essential this substance is to our very existence.

Most people living in our relatively sophisticated and technologically advanced communities are blissfully unaware, or uncaring, that an estimated 1.3 billion — yes, that's right, *billion* — men, women and children, mainly in Africa and Asia, have no access to safe drinking water. One of them dies every eight seconds from dehydration or a waterborne disease, which means that more than four million people die each year from the effects of unclean water. Water is the centre of their existence and often these poor souls are forced to walk miles to pick up polluted water daily from some watering hole or stream. This task largely falls to women and children. Most of them realize that wells could be drilled under their feet to produce potable water for all their needs but they lack the funds, know-how and equipment to do the job. To be able to turn on a tap and receive clean water, to take a shower, have a bath or do the laundry in good water is beyond the wildest hopes of those millions of woebegone people.

The definition of water is that it is a limpid, tasteless, odourless liquid compound of hydrogen and oxygen. A healthy human being has approximately 60% of their body weight composed of this wonderful substance and we are constantly losing a percentage of it, which must be replaced at a volume of somewhere around 64 ounces daily. Humans can survive many days without food, clothing, shelter, heat and the other things that are part of our daily lives, but after about four days without water, our life expectancy approaches nil.

Fresh water is essential also to global economies, which include manufacturing and commercial enterprises of all descriptions. Without it, the high-tech world would cease to exist and in fact, our world of today would expire. Water is indeed a fascinating subject as it governs our destiny. Control of clean water looms as probably the biggest challenge the world faces today. Yet, when the United Nations Universal Declaration of Human Rights was drafted over 50 years ago, water was not included in the list of protected rights because it was considered to be freely available like air. But times have changed. Despite everyday dependence on it, access to fresh water is far from equal or guaranteed. There is now an international community of organizations working towards building momentum for an international treaty that would guarantee the right to water. Among the recommendations of the UN's Committee on Economic,

Social and Cultural Rights, is the proviso to recognize water as a human right.

Interestingly, at both the 2nd World Water Forum held in 2000 in Holland and at the 3rd forum in Kyoto in 2004, Canada is on record as the only country to vote against a resolution by the UN Committee on Human Rights to appoint a Special Rapporteur to promote the right to drinking water. The Canadian delegation stated, "Canada does not accept that there is a right to drinking water and sanitation." It is probable our delegates were thinking of the USA's ongoing threat to Canadian water supplies.

Is there enough fresh water for everybody in the world? The answer is yes. Where is it? The Earth is a watery place. About 70% of the Earth's surface is water-covered. But water also exists in the air as water vapour and in the ground as soil moisture and in aquifers. Thanks to the water cycle, our planet's water supply is constantly moving from one place to another and from one form to another. The vast majority of water on the Earth's surface — over 98% — is saline water in the oceans. But it is the freshwater resources, such as water in streams, rivers, lakes and groundwater that provide people (and all life) with most of the water they need every day to live. Even though you may notice water on the Earth's surface, there is much more fresh water stored in the ground than there is in liquid form on the surface. In fact, some of the water you see flowing in rivers comes from seepage of groundwater into riverbeds. Water from precipitation continually seeps into the ground to recharge aquifers, while at the same time, water from underground aquifers continually recharges rivers through seepage.

As a matter of interest, a brief comment on the water cycle would not be amiss. It describes the existence and movement of water on, in and above the Earth. As mentioned, Earth's water is always in movement and is always changing states, from liquid to vapour to ice and back again. The water cycle has been working for billions of years and all life on Earth depends on it. Though there's no real starting point, we'll begin in the oceans, since that is where most of Earth's water exists. The sun, which drives the water cycle, heats water in the oceans. Some of it evaporates as vapour into the air. Ice and snow sublimate directly into water vapour. Rising air currents take the vapour up to the atmosphere, along with water from evapotranspiration, which is water transpired from plants and evaporated from the soil. The vapour rises into the air where cooler temperatures cause it to condense into clouds. Air currents move clouds and particles collide, join and fall out of the sky as precipitation. Some precipitation falls as snow and can accumulate as icecaps and glaciers. While present-day global warming seems to indicate some interruption of the water cycle, it's still too early to predict the environmental future with any accuracy.

There is much more to say about water, but space does not permit. Having in mind the background of human suffering, caused by scarce and impure water, the next time you lift a glass of our excellent quality water, you might give a thought to those millions of fellow travellers who are deprived of life's basics. While I'm not soliciting for funds, you may be interested to know that there are a number of sympathetic not-for-profit organizations that are busy creating water wells in countries where disease-ridden people cannot fend for themselves.

One such organization is called Lifewater Canada, a registered charity completely run by volunteers. They are dedicated to helping people in far-away countries who are in desperate need of fresh water. They have the equipment and know-how and have already created many wells that give hope to thousands of sick and dying people. This year, the organization is planning to drill sixty new wells in Liberia. Because of the volunteer nature of Lifewater Canada, wells can be completed for $3,000 each. There is a branch here in Vancouver, which can receive donations and issue income tax receipts. Pictorial evidence of onsite wells created is provided to all donors. Should any reader be interested, please refer to the author of this article for more information.

We have had some short-lived inconvenience in the Vancouver area due to polluted water, but our ability to boil water readily, and the availability of pure bottled water, pretty much prevented any health problems. We are very fortunate people.

How About Ice Cream

by A. John Ellis

Memories of eighty years ago include the exquisite joy of making our very own ice cream — children, quivering with excitement and gathered around the ice cream churn, each one clamouring for a turn on the crank, all keeping a watchful eye on the granulated river of lake ice, the coarse salt holding down the ice temperature as much as possible and the covering insulating blanket. After about an hour of fast churning, the carefully measured delicious ingredients were usually lightly frozen and it was time for testing and tasting. Off came the cover and out came the spoons. Breaths were held until a verdict was reached. *Eureka!* It was invariably a success and teamwork had produced a cooling, tasty, summertime treat fit for a queen. Ah, the simple pleasures of life never to be forgotten and mostly denied to modern generations.

Ice cream dates far back and there is much unproven folklore abounding about its early years. *The History of*

Ice Cream was written by the International Association of Ice Cream Manufacturers in 1978 and records some interesting items that are paraphrased in this article.

In the 17th century, Charles I of England hosted sumptuous state banquets that included many delicacies, but his greatest coup was achieved by his French chef who, on one occasion, had concocted a new dish, later to be repeated many times. It was cold, delicious and resembled fresh-fallen snow, but was unlike other conventional desserts of the day. Ice cream had been invented. Charles and his guests were delighted, so the king, wanting to ensure this new delicacy was served only at his table, tried to bribe the chef into maintaining complete secrecy about the ice cream recipe. It didn't work. The chef released the recipe. Incidentally, later in 1649, Charles, having fallen into disfavour, was beheaded.

Another story claims that the Roman Emperor Nero Claudius Caesar, used snow and ice to cool and freeze fruit drinks he enjoyed. Some time later, Marco Polo returned from his Far East journeys with a recipe for making water ices much like our present day sherbets. Marco Polo is also said to have seen ice cream made in China. He then introduced it to Italy. The myth continues with the Italian chefs of Catherine de' Medici taking the recipe for ice cream to France where she went to marry the Duc d'Orleans in 1533.

Moving well ahead, it is reported that Dolley Madison, wife of U.S. President James Madison, served ice cream at her husband's inaugural ball in 1813. Still later in 1851, commercial production of ice cream was started in North America in Baltimore, by Jacob Fussell, now considered to be the father of the American ice cream industry. In Canada, a Thomas Webb of Toronto, a confectioner, sold ice cream around 1850. William Neilson started selling ice cream in Toronto in 1893 and his company continued to do so for about the next one hundred years.

Over the years, ice cream has graduated from being a luxury item and has become the undoubted dessert of choice almost universally. Due to mass production techniques, it is readily and inexpensively available in most developed countries. Obviously, it can offer food for thought as well as being palate-pleasing. So, next time you are enjoying this delicacy, think back to Caesar, Marco Polo, Dolley Madison and all the others who originated and popularized it.

This year, Crofton Manor initiated 'ice cream socials' for the appreciative residents where a variety of ice cream treats were available from cones to floats to sundaes. This, no doubt reflecting the old childhood cry of "I scream, you scream, we all scream for ice cream." Hopefully the screaming will continue and fill us with nostalgia and calories to be worked off at the exercise classes and on the exercise machines!

Blueberries

by A. John Ellis

Did you know that a recent study by university researchers who analyzed sixty fruits and vegetables for their antioxidant capabilities gave blueberries the number one rating in their ability to destroy free radicals?

In case you are wondering — as I did — what in the dickens those are, free radicals contribute to many different diseases. In fact, a book could be written about them, but for simplicity's sake, let's just accept they are harmful things that invade our bodies and should be eschewed as much as possible.

Antioxidants are required to fight those wretched, unwelcome free radicals and blueberries enter the ring as odds-on favourites, being a powerhouse packed with antioxidants. They neutralize free radical damage to the collagen matrix of cells and tissues that can lead to cataracts, glaucoma, varicose veins, haemorrhoids, peptic ulcers, heart disease and cancer. They are said to help lower age-related macular degeneration and Alzheimer's disease or dementia.

It is also believed that eating lots of blueberries will significantly lessen brain damage from strokes and other neurological disorders. They contain an antioxidant compound, which blocks metabolic pathways that can lead to colon cancer. Wow! This all sounds like a hard sell for 'snake oil' but it isn't. Blueberries are Nature's gift to man, generally unsung and mistakenly avoided by many.

Beyond doubt, blueberries have remarkable and unique properties and they are delicious to boot. When the season rolled around, my late wife and I would purchase enough berries to last until the next year's crop became available. We consumed fresh berries while the season lasted and we froze the bulk for consumption during the coming year. They freeze readily and retain their flavour and characteristics throughout the year. Anyone who has an apartment-sized fridge can put away enough berries in the freezer compartment to last two people until next year's crop becomes available. We find that 48 one-pint square plastic containers do the trick. Consequently, every morning at breakfast, we ate blueberries with our porridge. We've done so for years. This is part of the reason why, even in my 98th year, only my bridge partners would dare suggest that my bidding indicates a touch of dementia. In fact, I know better. Thank you, blueberries!

For the statistically minded, it should be mentioned that one cup of blueberries contains 80 calories with no fat, cholesterol or sodium, has 5% carbohydrates, 20% fibre, 9 grams of sugar and 1 gram of protein plus 15% of the daily requirement of vitamin C. We have seen firsthand remarkable results in overweight people who followed a diet heavy in the berries and who stayed healthy and happy at the same time.

The berries can, of course, be used in many ways. They are a superb snack and dessert food; they are also delightful additions to cereals and salads. Mixed with other fruit in a blender, particularly bananas, they create a thirst-quenching and very tasty drink. They are also used to make fine jams, jellies and even wine.

As a matter of interest, BC produces about 95% of the Canadian production of cultivated blueberries, which is approximately 9 million kilograms per year. As well as local consumption, they enjoy an export trade, mainly to the USA, Europe, Japan and Australia.

By this time, you are probably aware I am a devoted long-time proponent of blueberry consumption. Right on. Why not join me by including the remarkable berry in your diet? You have nothing to lose and, I believe, much to gain!

Some Whys
of Japanese Longevity

by A. John Ellis

The Japanese lifespan is now the longest in the world. This raised the obvious question as to why this is so. In researching this question, I learned of an example of one Japanese gentleman who lived for almost 102 years and became a real role model who I'm sure most of us would like to emulate. He was Keizo Miura who, at one hundred years of age, was an athletic marvel. Daily, he ate a hearty breakfast, got into his tracksuit and raced through his indoor exercises. At the age of 99, he skied down Mont Blanc. In 1981, he became the oldest man to climb Mount Kilimanjaro, Africa's highest mountain. Keizo's son, at the age of 72, was the oldest man to reach the top of Mount Everest — the world's highest peak.

This father and son are only two examples from a growing and large number of extraordinarily fit Japanese seniors, who are statistically the healthiest in the world. Individually, they enjoy at least 75 years of good health exceeding the average for North Americans by some six years. Why is this so? It appears to be a question of diet and exercise. Their diet is vastly different from the typical Western diet and includes items to which the majority of Westerners pay scant attention at present. I would like to examine in some detail just one item amongst many, which contribute to Japanese good health. Namely tofu. For a long time it was relatively unknown to most of our Western populations, but now it is being recognized as a valuable addition to everyone's diet.

This nutritious food first appeared in China around 206 BC and was introduced into Japan in the Nara period (710–784 AD) by Japanese emissaries. They brought it back to Japan, along with teachings of Zen Buddhism, a doctrine, which prohibited the eating of meat or fish. Tofu became an important source of protein for the monks and priests in Japan's Buddhist temples. Gradually, the vegetarian cooking of the temples spread to the general population, came to be widely practiced and tofu has become a traditional Japanese food. It may be part of the reason for their very healthy senior population.

It is well-known that refined foods and sugar, in which the average North American overindulges, cause physical degeneration and disease as opposed to natural unrefined foods. Tofu falls in the latter category, but what exactly is tofu?

To produce the finished product, soybeans are soaked in water and mashed into a thick paste called 'go', which is then steamed and separated into soy milk and pulpy curds called 'okara'. A magnesium chloride compound taken from sea salt named 'nigara' is added to the soy milk to coagulate it into the soft mass known as tofu. Soybeans are extremely rich in protein, so much so that they are often referred to as the "meat of the field".

Tofu can be found in most Canadian food stores today. It comes in soft to firm varieties and in many different flavours. It can be eaten just as it is or together with savoury condiments and in other food additives. It is very adaptable and readily absorbs flavours. For instance, as a substitute for a conventional meat dish, tofu, served cold with a coating of yogurt makes a pleasant and highly nutritious change. Incidentally, at present tofu is low-priced when compared to most other proteins.

Over the years, Buddhist monks have believed that the consumption of tofu promotes good health and increased longevity. As previously mentioned, tofu is a part of the daily diet for many Japanese, both young and old, having been acknowledged as a pleasant-tasting source of vegetable proteins, lipids and minerals. It is also being consumed throughout most of Asia.

If you haven't tried tofu, a suggestion is to purchase a small block of the soft variety and eat it as is. If you find it palatable, then try experimenting with additives, especially organic vegetables. It also mixes well in soups and with meats and desserts of all descriptions. If you lack kitchen facilities, it is likely representations to a friendly catering department representative or a relative would not be amiss.

Having recounted all the foregoing, it is fully understandable that many seniors probably rate taste and comfort foods ahead of health foods, but if you do decide to give tofu a whirl, you don't need to set your sights on climbing Mount Everest — just plan to keep running or walking successfully away from the undertaker!

To substantiate the contention of the previous paragraph, quoting Hilaire Belloc's poem on "A matter of taste" is a fitting conclusion to this article:

Alas! What various tastes in food
Divide the human brotherhood!
Birds in their little nests agree
With Chinese, but not with me.
Colonials like their oysters hot,
Their omelets heavy — I do not,
The French are fond of slugs and frogs,
The Siamese eat puppy dogs.
...
And all the world is torn and rent
By varying views on nutriment.

Bon appetit and to your good health!

A Birthday Miscellany

by A. John Ellis

Many of us think about birthdays frequently. We read about them in the newspapers, hear about them on the radio and the TV, and are personally important. We celebrate family birthdays. I attended such a party the other day where it was more of less taken for granted there would be the usual cards, balloons, a cake, the singing of "Happy Birthday to You", toasts and all the other trimmings — and there were. Then I began to wonder about the history of birthdays, thinking there must be a lot more protocol and things to be said about birthdays beyond the simple ceremonies mentioned. So, I decided to do a little research on the subject.

Using trusty Google and Wikipedia on the internet, myriad facts about birthdays came to light, which are of considerable interest to me and maybe to you readers. A few of the facts are recited here and are believed to be correct, although some could be debatable.

Tradition has it that the birthday person, before blowing out the candles on a cake, should make a silent wish. If all candles are blown out with one breath, the wish is supposed to come true, but only if the person keeps the wish to her/himself. It is unusual for that person to cut the initial piece of cake. If the knife touches the bottom, or when withdrawn, comes out with pieces of cake adhering to it, he/she should kiss the nearest member of the opposite sex.

In the middle ages, the English baked birthday cakes and concealed symbolic items such as gold coins, thimbles, rings and other small metal objects in the cakes. A prediction was associated with each object and the practice is still extant today, although for hygienic and health considerations, it is no longer practiced by most thoughtful people. The predictions by the way, included that discovery of a gold coin would foretell great wealth and a person finding a thimble would never marry!

One statement from Wikipedia mentions that birthdays are not celebrated universally with some people preferring 'name day' celebrations (Valentine's day, Thanksgiving and the like). Another assertion states that Jehovah's Witnesses, for instance, do not celebrate either name days or birthdays, considering their origins to be pagan festivals along with Christmas and Easter. There is also another school of thought among people who loath to celebrate their birthdays as it reminds them that they are getting progressively older.

The *Happy Birthday* song tune is believed to be the most frequently sung melody in the world. Many countries have such songs in their own languages, for instance the French version is "Joyeux Anniversaire"; the

Spanish sing "Cumpleaños Feliz"; the Polish go "Sto lat"; the Dutch, "Lang zal hij/zij leven" and so on.

There are many 'notable' birthdays including for example one's 1st, 10th, 20th, 30th, 50th or 100th birthdays. Coming-of-ages often allow certain privileges and new responsibilities for the individual such as:

- 13th becoming a teenager
- 16th granting of drivers' licences in many jurisdictions
- 18th legal adult in many western countries
- 19th alcoholic beverage drinking age in Canada
- 20th legal age in some countries
- 21st alcoholic beverage drinking age in the USA
- 25th automobile rental permitted
- 35th age when individuals can run for the highest political office

There are birthstones named for each month of the year. Birthstones seem to have originated from Biblical times and reference is made to them in Exodus 39:10-14. There are also birth flowers and alternatives for each month, which are:

> January / Carnation
> February / Violet
> March / Daffodil
> April / Dahlia, Sweet Pea
> May / Sunflower, Lily of the Valley
> June / Rose, Honeysuckle
> July / Larkspur
> August / Lily, Gladiolus
> September / Forget-me-not, Morning Glory

October / Calendula (Marigold), Camellia
November / Chrysanthemum
December / Holly, Narcissus

The foregoing only scratches the surface of information on the subject of birthdays but space does not permit elaboration except to recount that racehorses traditionally celebrate their birthdays (that is, calculate their age in years) on August 1st in the southern hemisphere and on the January 1st in the northern hemisphere. I don't really believe that horses, race or otherwise, have a clue about their birthdays, but who am I to question Wikipedia?

Smiles and cheers to all — particularly when it is your birthday!

How About Automobiles?

by A. John Ellis

More than a hundred centuries ago, people started to move out of the caveman mode of living, which was basically to scrounge for whatever food nature and hunting provided, and they commenced growing crops. This agricultural activity, together with the discovery of the wheel, changed what had been a nomadic catch-as-catch-can way of living to a more settled existence, which in turn resulted in organized communities and educational facilities. This had a profound impact on population, allowing for steadily improving living conditions right up to the present day. The development of agriculture, can take a great deal of the credit for this. However, it has taken a hundred centuries to achieve our present lifestyle, which leads us to arguably the second-greatest achievement in the world, which has been accomplished in well under one century. That, of course, is the fast-track development of the automobile, which changed our way of life and the configuration of the developed world forever. There have been many other great strides made in technology affecting our lives favourably, but none have equalled the development of the automobile, which altered our way of living in very short order.

In Richard A. Wright's book *West of Laramie*, it says:

> We reserve for the car an emotional relationship we do not have with other machines, not with refrigerators, or airplanes or even the curiously human computer. The car has been venerated as an object of affection, excitement, even love. And when it fails us, we heap upon it the bitterness and intense anger we generally reserve for our loved ones.
>
> The automobile is, like no other machine, a part of us. Think for a moment about the world of 100 years ago. Travel was slow and difficult. A trip to anywhere was a major undertaking. Dearborn was a day's journey from Detroit on the road to Chicago. Most roads were just gravel or dirt. Cities, usually built on streams or lakes or rail lines were compact and congested. They were quickly transformed by the car into sprawling urban complexes, held together — and in some ways split apart — by the freeways and interstates that in fact bind them.
>
> Buildings have been razed and farmland paved over to provide parking for the almost

> 300 million vehicles we own in the United States alone.
>
> And along those roads are motels, fast-food restaurants, shopping malls, drive-in movies, drive-in banks, drive-in florists, even drive-in funeral homes.
>
> In this century, the automobile has spawned whole industries where none were before.
>
> Auto makers are the biggest or among the biggest consumers of steel, aluminum, copper, glass, zinc, leather, plastic and platinum and they use most of the lead and rubber consumed in the United States.

The automobile has made an immense impact upon our lives. For some materially-conscious people, the automobile has become a status symbol, although this misguided philosophy is gradually dissipating. Let's take a look back at how it all started.

In 1885, Karl Benz of Germany produced the first internal-combustion-powered three-wheeled car, put it into production, and people bought it. Years earlier, a Frenchman named Nicolas Cugnot had fitted a wagon with a steam engine and, while it ran, it was impractical, whereas Benz' creation was usable. At that time, unknown to one another, there were many mechanically-minded individuals working on motorized vehicle inventions. Well-known names appeared like Daimler in Germany, Renault and Peugeot in France, and Olds, Buick and Ford in the USA. In the UK, British Daimler was founded in 1896, and the British have since produced great cars like

Bentleys, Jaguars, Rolls Royces and others. Incidentally, in Germany, the Daimler and Benz companies joined forces to become Mercedes-Benz in 1926 and have been producing high-quality, much sought-after automobiles ever since.

Since those early days, automobile designs and production have made great strides and manufacturers have produced better and better vehicles at prices within the reach of the masses. The greatest contribution was undoubtedly Henry Ford's creation of the assembly-line production of the famous Model 'T'. Other carmakers emulated his techniques and production generally increased rapidly with a few setbacks here and there with the odd bankruptcy occurring in one-time popular makes.

One has only to observe the passing traffic flows to appreciate the vastness of the car market. Cars of every description, some with roots in foreign countries, continually stream by in the hundreds and thousands, depending on the location. It would gladden the hearts of all those early pioneers of the industry to witness these processions, which will undoubtedly carry on and on worldwide with less and less atmospheric pollution as the years unfold. It is reasonable to predict that eventually automobiles will create zero pollution while the necessity for people's mobility will probably remain at least constant.

Like many other types of antique collectors, it is not surprising that there are increasingly large numbers of antique car buffs both solo and formed into associations. They have a wealth of material to draw from and lovingly put countless hours into restoring old vehicles to their original running state, which takes a lot of ingenuity in finding or duplicating parts and much hard work. It is certainly an exciting and rewarding hobby, one which gives onlookers a taste of years gone by whenever there is a rally or when visiting an antique car museum or collection.

Just such a rally is being planned at Crofton Manor for an afternoon in June this year. Residents and friends will be treated to a display of antique cars on the parking lot. The proud owners will be on hand to discuss their handiwork and to answer questions. It is probable the 'Royal Car' will be exhibited — a 1939 Buick, which has transported all the royals, including the Queen and the Duke, who have visited Vancouver in recent years.

It will be a fun and nostalgic gala — don't miss it!

Elspeth & Company

by A. John Ellis

Elegant she wasn't, but she had character and, when shown respect and a lot of tender loving care, she exuded a certain charm. Age was catching up with her and she was full of creaks and groans, but she still had the strength to break a person's arm when put to the test. Race, creed and language were matters of complete indifference to Elspeth. She was black as the ace of spades, and this only added to her charm as she steadfastly tried to carry on as she had done in her youth.

Elspeth was my first automobile and I have never forgotten her — a 1927 Model 'T' Ford coupe. The last year of the 'T' production was 1927. Production had started on October 1, 1908 and over the next 19 years, Ford built 15,000,000 automobiles with the Model 'T' engine and I was the proud owner of one of them!

Our world was in the grips of a severe depression in the early "Dirty Thirties" and money was scarce, but like most eager teenagers, I had a burning desire to become road-borne with wheels of my own. And there she was — Elspeth — a black beauty standing on the floor of an automobile dealer's showroom on St. Catherine Street in Montreal. Dared I hope? Somewhat timidly, I entered, surveyed and patted my dream machine. "Is she in good working order?" I asked the floor salesman. He of course answered the anticipated question in a strong affirmative. Next dreaded question — how much?

"Twenty dollars," he replied.

"Too much," I countered, "but I'll give you fifteen dollars if you can arrange and include a driver's licence for me."

To my joy, he agreed and said I was to return the next day to take delivery of the car and the licence.

Driving away from the dealer's showroom, I felt I must be the luckiest guy in the world until I reached a major intersection and Elspeth stalled and would not restart. Fortunately, a sympathetic motorist gave us a nice push-start. Our luck held until we wheeled into my home driveway. The trouble was that the radiator was empty and the engine had overheated, but that was only the beginning of a series of mechanical difficulties, which I found challenging. These lasted until I sold Elspeth for twenty dollars to a friend about two years later. We still remained friends. He was actually the one who christened her 'Elspeth' and so felt he had a responsibility for her.

The trials of keeping Elspeth roadworthy for two years resulted in making me a competent amateur mechanic, which has been very useful ever since. The problem of obtaining required spare parts to keep the coupe on the road was solved by buying two Model 'T' chassis at five dollars a piece and cannibalizing them as occasion demanded. It worked and very well too — with Elspeth responding to the careful care and with gasoline selling at eleven cents a gallon we were able to build up several thousand miles of easy-on-the-pocketbook happy driving.

One of the main objectives in keeping Elspeth road-worthy was to ensure safety, so the brakes and running gear required special attention. It was good training and, during my ownership, we had no accidents. Of course, traffic was much lighter in those days and it was perhaps easier to observe the rules of the road than it is today with the roads crowded with risk-taking drivers.

I'll not take further time discussing Elspeth, other than to say it was one of the most enjoyable and instructive periods of my life when I learned, in short order, a great deal about mechanics and the art of negotiating. I think a few words about the Model 'T' and Henry Ford would not be amiss.

Henry's business plan was to buy, for cash, tremendous quantities of raw materials, thereby obtaining very low prices and then producing well-made quality cars in hitherto unheard of numbers at rock-bottom prices. He established efficient assembly-line production and the operation quickly became highly successful.

The following advertisement appeared in *Life Magazine* on October 1st, 1908:

FORD HIGH PRICED QUALITY IN A LOW PRICED CAR
The Ford Four Cylinder, Twenty Horse Power, Five Passenger Touring Car $850.00 Fob Detroit.

> We defy anyone to break a Ford Vanadium steel part with any test or strain less than 50% greater than is required to put any other special automobile steel entirely out of business.

Another excerpt from a sales brochure:

> The Model 'T' is built entirely of the best materials obtainable. No car at $5,000 has higher grade, for none can be bought. Heat treated Ford Vanadium steel.
>
> Nobody disputes that Vanadium steel is the finest steel obtainable...

By 1914, the Model 'T' was selling so well, Ford saw little reason to spend much on advertising. The company dropped most of its ads in national magazines that year and, in 1917, halted paid advertising altogether. He did not buy any more ad space for the Model 'T' until 1923.

"You can paint it any colour, so long as it's black." It has never been proven that this quote — attributed to Henry Ford — was actually said by him, but it survived for 75 years and does indicate something about America's beloved Model 'T' — its 'steadfastness', its enduring and endearing 'sameness'. It is a fact that for most of the years of Model 'T' production the only colour offered was black. The principal reason for this was that the black enamel used dried more quickly than other paint and therefore sped up production.

While all this is now ancient history, there is no question that Henry Ford created the car of the century and succeeded in his quest to build a car for the masses. Many new Ford designs and models followed the Model 'T' and the company is still flourishing, but anyone in America who can recall the early part of the twentieth century probably has a special place in his/her heart for the Model 'T'.

Gadgetry Worship

by A. John Ellis

There are many types of love that motivate individuals and society.

We all know about puppy love, family love, romantic love, love of money (*i.e.*, material love), love of fame and recognition, love of sports, love of food, love of alcohol and drugs and so on, *ad infinitum*, but probably the most pernicious but harmless of all these, particularly in America, is the love for automobiles and accompanying gadgetry.

By the way of illustration, I should like to cite the rivalry between the proud owners of a 'top-of-the-line' Cadillac and a late-model Rolls-Royce. They were both vying for the best array in accessories and did not wish to be outclassed in any way.

Quotes from one of their recent meetings are as follows:

Caddy owner ('CO') to Rolls owner ('RO'):

CO: "You got a telephone in your car?"
RO: "Of course."
CO: "You got a teletype machine?"
RO: "Of course."
CO: "You got a computer?"
RO: "Yes."
CO: "Are you on high-speed internet?"
RO: "Of course."
CO: "And a bar and TV with 200 channels?"
RO: (becoming somewhat petulant) "Yes, yes."
CO: "You got a double bed installed?"
RO: (crestfallen) "No, *dammit*!!!"

They parted company at this juncture, whereupon the Rolls owner went straight to his mechanic and asked him to install a double bed in his car immediately, which was done.

Triumphant, the Rolls owner sought out the Caddy owner the next morning, finding him parked on a side street with all the windows clouded up, so he rapped on a window, which produced an irate Caddy owner who lowered the window and poked his head out with a towel wrapped around his neck.

CO: "Now what do you want?"
RO: "I just want to let you know I now have a double bed installed in my jolly superior Rolls Royce."
CO: "You mean to say, just to tell me *that*, you got me out of my shower?!?"

Technology Musings

by A. John Ellis

For those of us born in the early 1900s, science and technology have been predominant in our lifestyles and we have seen tremendous changes in practically everything appertaining to life's hardware. Can these people look back and say in all honesty that they were 'the good old days'? You be the judge.

Without the amazing advances made in technical areas, how would the world's population, which has gone from one billion five hundred million to approximately six-and-one-half billion in about one hundred years, sustain itself? It can be argued that without the strides made in access to medical and life-sustaining products, the enormous increase in population would not have occurred, but that is conjecture only and we are dealing with the here and now as well as a glimpse backward.

Pragmatically, let's look at a few of the phenomenal changes in lifestyles that have taken place during the last century and that are predominant in the minds of the doers and onlookers of that period.

At the beginning of the twentieth century, horse-drawn vehicles were the accepted means of transportation and, in Canada, we thrilled to the tinkle of sleigh bells in the snow and the crunch of sleigh runners in the crisp atmosphere. About the only reminder left of those days is to watch the now-ancient film *White Christmas* with Bing Crosby, who passed away some years ago. In North America, the era of the internal combustion engine was ushered in mainly by Henry Ford and his Model 'T'. The world generally followed suit and has never looked back with slick, powerful, fast and comfortable automobiles now being the order of the day, along with millions of kilometres of asphalt highways and urban roads traversing most advanced countries and cities. The urge, or perhaps the necessity, to be continually somewhere else pervades the people's actions and has resulted in air pollution of massive and life-threatening proportions, particularly so in urban centres. It is contended that the vexatious problem of climate change is the result of this and other related factors.

The same thing has occurred in air transportation. Flimsy wood, cloth and wire flying machines have made steady progress to where we now take for granted magnificent aeroplanes, which transport millions of people globally in comparative safety at great speeds and comfort.

In the fields of medicine, beneficial drugs and patient treatments have been advanced to a point where, at least in the Western World and in parts of Asia, longevity has been steadily climbing and one hundred plus years of age is no longer of phenomenon. There is no question that science and technology have brought about this encouraging state.

Another field that has been steadily improving, thanks to knowledge, is agriculture. It's providing the necessary sustenance to take care of the majority of six-and-a-half billion hungry people, although there are admittedly millions of fellow travellers on the brink of starvation. The latter are mostly victims of graft, bad planning and ineffective governments.

The list goes on and on, but unquestionably the twentieth century highlighted human ingenuity with awe-inspiring technical and scientific achievements. One area not yet mentioned in this article is communications. This is a huge field and so I will only highlight a minuscule area. Namely, the touch-tone telephone, which will be treated in a facetious manner with serious undertones.

Most people using touch-tone telephones have experienced the frustration of trying to speak with a human being when seeking help, appointments or information. We seem to be in the clutches of impersonal technology and often, having gone through the canned voice instructions getting us to press numbers 1 to 9, we end up with a request to wait for a service representative, which may take some time as they are all busy looking after other customers. Meanwhile, we are entertained with music of their choice. So we slam down the receiver!

Recently, a well-known pharmacy has adopted the touch-tone procedure to fill renewal prescriptions. Will we be allowed to die without referring to a touch-tone telephone? How far is this thing going to go? For example a bit of good humour fantasy:

"Hello, Heaven? Are you willing to receive me?"

Answer:
"Press 1 if you are dying in English." to which you comply followed by other instructions:-
"Press 2 if you wish to be cremated."
"Press 3 if you want a memorial service."
"Press 4 if you require transportation."
"Press 5 if you wish to be given last rites."
"Press 6 if you wish to speak to someone in our Transmission Department, but as all Service Representatives are busy serving other would-be clients, it could be a long wait. Meanwhile, you will be entertained by a rendition of "Amazing Grace". If you are in a great hurry, you can go to our competition where we know you will receive an immediate and very warm welcome!"

Amen!

Our Global Village

by A. John Ellis

What comes to mind when the following figures are stated?

One billion six hundred million
One billion nine hundred million
Two billion five hundred million
Four billion
Six billion two hundred million

No, they do not represent baseball, basketball, football or hockey players' salaries, or chief executive or Hollywood stars' incomes, or national deficits or debts. Actually, as some readers have no doubt guessed, those figures are the world's population starting in 1900 AD and moving up by twenty-five year intervals.

It had taken from the beginning of time to 1900 AD for the world's population to reach one billion, six hundred million, but almost in the twinkling of an eye, the population had skyrocketed to six billion two hundred million. It has quadrupled in one century — in the lifetime of some people who are still with us — and is still increasing. Canada's, through immigration and births, approximately tripled over the same period. Checking on the internet, it is recorded that as of 10th August, '03, the actual world population was 6,302,486,405. It is absolutely mind-boggling.

Interestingly and incidentally, of the approximately six billion people, some four billion are in Asian countries where it is estimated that 65% of all commercial transactions in the world are being processed.

While the population explosion has been occurring, man has made fantastic technological strides in all manner of ways including transportation and communications. As a result, the term 'global village' has become an accepted reality.

Living in the undoubted luxury of Crofton Manor, it is hard to envision the chaotic lifestyles endured by a large percentage of the world's people, but it is a very real situation, which seems likely to worsen. By the year 2050, extrapolated figures place the population at 9,084,495,405! I, by the way, would be happy to take all bets that this figure will not be achieved. (Just try to collect.)

We read almost daily of the dire consequences humanity is having on the environment and natural resources. It would seem we are collectively crushing nature to death and leaving a fearsome legacy for our offspring if something drastic is not done, or occurs, to rectify the damage being done by our profligate ways. It seems nature is fighting back in many ways, such as fatal diseases like AIDS, Ebola, and SARS, wars, terrorism, plagues, pestilences, droughts, famine, floods, riots, major temperature changes and the like; but is so far, losing the battle. There has also been the suggestion that there may be a major asteroid collision in the relatively near future, which would have a salutary effect on our population, as may have happened in the dinosaur era.

Corrective action can be undertaken and it is up to governments to institute such action, backed by the citizens. It should start with a concerted drive to reverse the population increase, which is the real culprit in our troubled existence. China, for example, with its one-child policy made a valiant effort but it's not without its problems, and sadly, it seems this vexatious problem has been swept under the carpet in other jurisdictions, and it should not be allowed to continue this way. There is no sense in throwing up our hands and saying nothing can be done about mankind's drive to reproduce.

The United Nations would be a good place to institute action and, on the grassroots level, we should all be lobbying our politicians and anyone else who will listen to face up to this very real problem. We could maybe take some comfort in the fact that in industrialized countries, as the infancy mortality rate goes down and the gps increases, birth rates tend to go down, but this is not enough.

While a bit of an oxymoron, nature may produce a population-reducing agent that will defy human ingenuity to counter.

These are highly controversial thoughts, which will no doubt raise a lot of hackles and meet with considerable opposition. Please think about it and talk it over with your friends and contacts and write to your government representatives if you agree with the thesis. Who knows? The ripple effect could turn into a gigantic tidal wave, and that just sounds like what we need.

Hey Hey Shorties

by A. John Ellis

The amazing online world of the internet, carries a dissertation on 'heightism', which, as far as I can determine, is a coined word that cannot be found in any of my dictionaries. This unusual word, according to Wikipedia, translates into a form of discrimination based on height. In principle, it can refer to unfavourable treatment of either unusually tall or short people.

I belong to the latter group at the top end of the short category, which I recall is listed somewhere as those who are between five-foot-four and five-foot-seven. I find, as I believe most people do, that because of the inexorable march of time, I have shrunk considerably but fortunately, I can still see over most counters without a prop. Also I can't agree that lack of altitude has ever resulted in my receiving unfavourable treatment except perhaps the occasional gibe from some massive hunk of tall, stupid male referring to me as 'shorty'. I used to put a stop to that by stamping hard on the instep of the offender and beating a hasty retreat — usually there was no repetition of the implied criticism. So, I'll share with you the positive and sometimes humourous side of a shorty's travel through time and other related material.

In the Canadian Football League, it's great to watch some very fleet-of-foot five-foot-six-short running backs regularly leaving two to three-hundred-pound giants in their wake. In my early days, I looked forward to playing the game big time, but had to compromise by playing scrum half in English rugby leagues both in Canada and in England during WWII. For those unaware of the game, I should explain that scrum halves are generally shorties and for me it was a pleasure and good fun — except for the odd concussion!

In other sporting activities, I found myself to be a natural at skiing, and notably, in competitive events, lack of height stood shorties in good stead. I recall in the thirties competing in a tough downhill race (le Kandahar at Mont-Tremblant, Quebec) when some tall skiers went off-course on a particularly steep schuss, wound them-selves around trees and ended up with broken legs. I also had trouble with that part of the course and took a bad tumble but, being built close to the ground, merely bounced a few times and merrily went on to finish the race in a respectable bronze category time.

Learning to fly aircraft, again during the thirties, I found the old crates' cockpits ideal for shorties, though tall people had difficulties keeping their heads down out of the slipstream. For them, it was especially miserable when flying a machine equipped with one of the old castor oil spewing engines — holdovers from WWI long since disappeared, of course. Anyway, another positive for shorties.

While on the subject of flying, I should mention that for business and cultural reasons, post-war, I needed to travel millions of miles, mostly in remarkable and sleek aircraft, the development of which had been fast-forwarded by the war. Beautiful to behold but, alas, for economic reasons, the airlines often skimped on the seating configurations to the discomfort of passengers, particularly on long flights. While the six-foot-plus types were constantly wondering where to park their knobbly knees, we shorties were scoring again — with comfort, not the flight attendants!

Come World War II, I found myself chasing the enemy across Europe and back into Germany. Whenever fighting movement became static, our opponents would set up enfilade machine-gun fire, which left me unscathed — I like to believe they thought all Canadians were six feet or taller and they set their sweep accordingly. Consequently, the bullets passed harmlessly over my head instead of into it. Another plus for shorties.

Then came peace and back to business. Standing around with a bunch of six-footers had its disadvantages, but sitting at a conference or boardroom table evened the score. In the post-war days when smoking was a way of life rather than death, the so-called social side of business, in which I was involved, played a ridiculously important role. Cocktail parties were *de rigueur* and you missed one at peril of perhaps losing some business. I well remember a prominent cardiologist in Montreal telling me he thought the business crowd were stupid to attend a smoke-filled and booze-ridden atmosphere at cocktail parties, usually after a stressful day. He predicted our early demise from lung cancer or liver troubles. He said we would be much better advised instead, in the interest of longevity, to go home, put on our slippers, relax and drink a modest highball with our wives. However, I ignored the advice and attended every party possible, partly because of my suspected immunity from his dire predictions. You see I would stand around, drink in hand, talking to waistcoat buttons — three-piece suits were also then in vogue — at which level, the air was much purer. So far, I have escaped lung cancer whereas many of my taller, party-going acquaintances have since succumbed to the disease. As far as the ladies were concerned, a few tall, well-endowed but willowy business professionals, waving long black silver-decorated cigarette holders, were usually on hand at the parties and I found standing and talking with them also had its points. So another score for shorties.

I mentioned at the opening of this article that the 'short' category included people between five-foot-four and five-foot-seven inches. Where this originated, I have no idea, but I wonder how people on either side are categorized? I suggest maybe 'squirt' and 'behemoth' with no offence to either intended.

In any event, as I am concentrating on shorties, maybe the many short notorious notables who have graced or are gracing this planet will be encouraging to my ilk. For instance, President Vladimir Putin of Russia is five-foot-five and Joseph Stalin was five-foot-five along with Francisco Franco at five-foot-four. French President Nicholas Sarkozy, who made a state visit to the UK in March of 2008, received much attention from the press reporters who were uncommonly united in passing comment on the fact that he is a short man who wore sizeable heels on his shoes in contrast to the flat shoes worn by his taller wife, Carla Bruni. Ludwig Beethoven, was five-foot-six. T.E. Lawrence of Arabia was five-foot-five-and-a-half, and so were Marilyn Monroe and Horatio Nelson. Woody Allen and Aristotle Onassis checked in at five-foot-five, with Pablo Picasso and Mae West measuring five-foot-four. Micky Rooney, Sammy Davis Jr. and Judy Garland were all five-foot-three, with Mary Pickford an even five feet, edging out Dolly Parton who is four-foot-eleven. I could recite the names of dozens more international celebrities who are, or were, short and shorter than the listed names, but the point is that to be successful, height is of little consequence.

All the foregoing seems to indicate that the wonderful world of opportunity, is open to all of us — irrespective of physical dimensions.

Patio Gardening

by A. John Ellis

Roses are red,
Violets are blue
Fresh veggies are mostly green
And very good for you — too!

That rather sad time of the year had arrived bringing cool, wet weather and spelling *au revoir* to the jaunty flowers and vegetable plants that had given us a lot of joy and food during the excellent growing season of 2002. As I put most of our miniature garden to bed for yet another year, I reflected on the past couple of years since our move to Crofton Manor on April 1, 2000.

My wife and I had been happy and enthusiastic gardeners for several decades. One of our biggest regrets on moving to this fine retirement home was that we would have to abandon our principal and thoroughly enjoyable hobby — gardening. She got a great deal of pleasure in landscaping our spacious grounds and growing flowers while I grew a variety of vegetables in two different plots, which supplied us with plentiful crops throughout the year, including the winter months for certain hardy types. A side benefit to these activities was of course, the exercise we derived in the open air while teaming with nature.

When the turmoil of moving from a 6,000-square-foot house to a relatively small suite had subsided, the patio — approximately 10'×4' — caught my eye. With an eastern exposure and several hours of morning sunshine, I thought it could be a candidate for an intensive compact garden. So why not give it a whirl? I did, and have been agreeably surprised with the results.

As we prepare our own lunches, fresh pesticide-free vegetables are always welcome. This year, we enjoyed about two months of lettuce, green beans and green onions, as well as arugula, an assortment of herbs and well over a hundred cherry tomatoes, which ripened very satisfactorily in the superb summer weather we enjoyed this year. We also harvested two crops of sugar snap peas and curly cress. The first year we tried kale with only modest success. At the time of writing (early October), we have a good crop of onions maturing and awaiting the first heavy frost.

A most colourful and all-around pleasing centrepiece for a patio garden is scarlet runner beans. They are easy to grow and invariably live up to their catalogue description — "large sprays of beautiful scarlet flowers stand out from this vine that is really lovely on balconies and trellises." These delightful plants can be started as seedlings indoors and transplanted outdoors as soon as there is no threat of frosts. They mature in about 75 days, so seedlings started in March will start producing in late May or early June. Seeds, of course, can be planted directly into the soil as soon as the last frost has occurred, delaying the harvesting by a few weeks.

Lettuce can be grown from seeds, as described above, or from seedlings readily available at nurseries and grocery stores. Eight heads of mixed romaine and leafy types will produce masses of salad material provided the heads are not uprooted with only the leaves picked as required.

Besides vegetables, a few flowering plants provide additional colour and we have found impatiens — particularly New Guinea impatiens — are very satisfactory, requiring only water with occasional doses of Miracle-Gro (or similar 15-30-15) and no 'dead-heading'. They bloom profusely all summer.

All the above can be grown in pots and planters using readily available potting soil. We have found the rectangular plastic containers, available in many sizes from gardening stores, to be very satisfactory. While pots and containers can be placed at floor level, it is preferable to locate them about 16" off the floor — easily arranged with plywood planks and, for instance, empty 17-litre plastic buckets for props.

A lot more could be written about this subject but, suffice to say, while enjoying the happy lifestyle at Crofton Manor, we have found an unexpected and enjoyable outlet for our gardening zest — a miniature garden with little expense, not too much TLC and no lawns to mow!

Schultz

by A. John Ellis

To him, life was the proverbial bowl of cherries, although he would have preferred hamburger if in fact a bowl of anything was being offered. He was forever looking for fun and he loved to play simple games, often of his own making, with the object of outwitting his opponent. Very much a member of the family, when time hung heavily and there was nothing better to do, he would climb into a made-up bed, get under the coverlet with head on the pillow, and snatch a few minutes sleep complete with snores and doubtless happy dreams.

Schultz was a large, shorthaired dachshund with a sparkling personality, a permanently happy-go-lucky frame of mind and an apparent conviction that he was human and destined to entertain the gang. He was also aggressively protective of our home to our occasional embarrassment, when some innocent person received a sharp nip on the ankle for daring to set foot on our property.

We were in Halifax, Nova Scotia when Schultz adopted us and quickly became the life of the party for several years both there and in Westmount, Quebec. In Halifax, we were looking for a mature, pleasant and domesticated dog. His owners assured us he would be an excellent companion for our children but omitted to tell us he was the scourge of their neighbourhood due to his strong family protection instincts. By the time we realized this fact, which had flowed through to our family, he had endeared himself to all of us and we could not think seriously of parting company. Our memories of him some forty years later are as fresh now as they were then, and a recitation follows a small selection of vignettes of his enthusiastic antics.

Family picnics were a regular feature of our lives where Schultz became front and centre in activities. Often we would travel to a picnic site by boat, which he found rather tiresome as he didn't like being confined and he always wanted to be the first off the boat. Consequently, when nearing home on the return journey, he would try, prematurely, to leap onto the dock, often as not landing in the water. Swimming was not one of his strong points and he gradually sank bottom down with just his nose above water and making no progress towards land. He required rescuing on several occasions.

He regularly chased seagulls and sandpipers with joyous abandon but never caught one. It seemed he thought he could run on water and as a result, having plunged at full-tilt beyond his depth, would find himself struggling to make landfall while being taunted by swooping gulls who thoroughly enjoyed his predicament.

Schultz was a softie too. We had a mother cat who was nursing several kittens when she was on the losing end of a fight with an unknown assailant who mangled her so badly that she was forced to abandon her kittens. Schultz, on his own initiative, took over cuddling, licking and mothering the little ones, while we supplied warm milk until the crisis was over. All concerned survived — thanks mainly to him.

As mentioned, he liked to play little games, which he originated. Our house in Westmount had a staircase to the second floor at each end of a long corridor, and when someone would start up one staircase, Schultz would rush up the other one and run fast as he could along the second floor corridor in the hope that he would arrive at the head of the other staircase before that someone made it to the top. There, he would stand gleefully wagging his tail as if to say, "Ha ha, I beat you." He usually did.

The greetings he gave family members arriving home were something to behold. When the front door opened and one of us stepped inside, Schultz, who would have been waiting at the rear of the corridor, would race up the highly polished floor, put on the brakes too late and crash into that family member — sometimes with rather devastating results, as he weighed about twenty-six pounds. There was, however, no denying the sincere warmth of this welcome home!

There were many other episodes perhaps worth recounting, but space does not permit and a few very brief comments about the breed may be of interest.

Paraphrasing from an article by Steven Michelson, dachshunds are described as "characters", comically cute to look at, both in their unique physical proportions and also in their spirited antics, always wanting to be included in everything. They were originally bred to hunt badgers in Germany in the 18th and 19th centuries. Brought to America in 1887, they enjoyed varying degrees of popularity. Because of the world wars, particularly WWI, they were innocent victims of much hostility.

Schultz was a real character and lots of fun. We still miss him.

Mary Pack — Founder of The Arthritis Society

by C. Joan Ellis

Having served as a volunteer for many years and, subsequently, six years as a member of the board of the Arthritis Society with Mary Pack, we became good friends and she frequently visited my home where I grew a variety of flowers in my gardens. Mary's favourite colour was blue and, every spring and early summer, I had a large and colourful display of bluebells, which she found very pleasing. I expect it reminded her of the symbolic Arthritis Society bluebirds.

Bluebell bulbs are hardy, transplant readily and multiply rapidly, so Mary asked if she could have some of the bulbs, which I was delighted to supply. These, she planted somewhere on the society's property on West 7th Avenue in Vancouver where I understand they initially flourished. Perhaps they have survived to this day.

Bluebells and bluebirds of happiness aside, Mary Pack was unquestionably the right person at the right time. Her interest in aiding victims of arthritis in all its forms stemmed from her school teaching days. She saw many young people severely handicapped by the malady, with nowhere to turn for relief, and she determined to create a facility to ease their suffering. She had the organizing skills backed by forceful persuasion and soon, the embryonic society was underway. The rest is history and I only wish that Mary could switch on the internet today, to witness what her handiwork is producing internationally. She would not take 'no' for an answer and she gave no thought to self-aggrandizement or personal monetary gain. In this latter respect, she was awarded a grant of $50,000 by the Royal Bank, which I understood she intended to use largely for the benefit of the society. I remonstrated with her, saying she should think of herself occasionally. Her reply: "I'm doing what I want to do, thank you."

Mary Pack was a truly great powerhouse lady, who has benefitted mankind as few others have done.

Visit to Campbell River BC 1967

by C. Joan Ellis

Along the shore, beneath the pines,
To see the Kwakiutl nation
We all went in friendly fashion,
Along the shore, beneath the pines.

No noble chieftain came to greet us
No angry savage tried to scalp us
Along the shore, beneath the pines,
No wigwam there, but just a store.

Along the shore, beneath the pines,
Members of first nations sitting in the sun
Dark, gentle eyes and peaceful calm,
Along the shore, beneath the pines.

Shibuya & Hachiko

by C. Joan Ellis

Post-World War II, my husband and I made countless trips to Japan and it fast became our favourite country to visit. While cultural and business meetings took us to many parts of the country, we tended to spend a lot of time in the fascinating city of Tokyo.

Through Japanese friends, we gradually began to learn of a number of interesting things about Japan's folklore and culture as well as becoming well-acquainted with the various areas of Tokyo. One of the areas is Shibuya.

Described as being vibrant, lively, fun, faddish, crowded, cramped, and busy, Shibuya is a shopping and entertainment district in the west of the city. It has many large department stores — one of which is Tokyu Hands, founded by a now-deceased good friend of ours who took great pride in giving us a tour of this fabulous specialty store on one of our trips. Shibuya is also the location of both the NHK studios — Japan's broadcasting and TV network — and 1964 Olympic Gymnasium. Of even greater interest, is the statue of Hachiko that stands at an exit of the Shibuya Railway Station and thereby hangs a sad tale of unsurpassed canine loyalty.

Hachiko was a white male Akita dog born in Odate, Japan in November 1923. When two months old, he went to the home of Professor Eizaburo Ueno, a Tokyo University teacher living in the Shibuya district. They became fast friends.

Every morning, Hachiko walked with his friend to the Shibuya railway station where they parted company. Hachiko went home and Dr. Ueno went by train to teach at the university. In the evening, the routine was reversed, the Professor always found Hachiko waiting for him. On May 21, 1925, Dr. Ueno suffered a stroke and died at the university. Hachiko waited that evening until the last train had arrived and he continued to do so for ten years until he died at the station on March 7, 1934.

The newspapers recorded Hachiko's faithful vigil and he became very famous. A life-sized statue was erected at the station and has become a favourite meeting place. Each year on March 7th, a festival is organized in front of Hachiko's statue to honour his memory. His body rests in the National Science Museum.

Teddy Bears

by A. John Ellis

'Benevolence' can be described in a wide variety of ways including: God's grace, goodwill, unselfishness, loving kindness, kind feelings, goodness of heart, sympathy, love, consideration, and other related sentiments.

We have a large amount of benevolence being practicably demonstrated here in Crofton Manor by the group of resident ladies who are knitting attractive teddy bears for presentation to handicapped and deprived children. It is a wonderful project, which will bring lifetime joy into the lives of many children who would otherwise have never imagined receiving a cuddly teddy bear due to the benevolence of complete, but caring, strangers. Our knitters deserve a vote of warmest congratulations.

Many adults have very fond recollections of their teddy bears, who gave them comfort in times of childhood stress, gave them companionship, particularly at bedtime, and always lent a sympathetic ear to all troubles, real or imagined. While they may not wish to admit it, some adults still keep the old teddy bear close at hand in their bedrooms.

The teddy bear craze is not so very old, dating back to US President Theodore Roosevelt, who was appointed on September 14th, 1901 following the assassination of William McKinley.

Theodore Roosevelt, nicknamed 'Teddy', enjoyed big-game hunting. Legend has it that the teddy bear had its birth in Colorado, when after an unsuccessful day's hunt, the maids at the hotel where he was staying, presented him with a miniature stuffed fabric bear by way of consolation. There are also other versions but suffice to say teddy bears over the years to date can call the late president 'father'.

The aura of the teddy bear has spread worldwide. For instance today there are teddy bear magazines in Australia, Canada, Germany, Japan, the UK, and doubtless other countries as well. There are also teddy bear clubs and events operating in many countries. Books have been written about the phenomenal make-believe creature who has captured the fancy of generations globally and with good reason.

Occasional escape from reality in this often harsh and violent world can be therapeutic for young and old alike.

So a resounding thank you to all teddy bears!

Singing Notes

by A. John Ellis

Mrs. Leora Williams, the talented pianist who leads our Crofton Manor Glee Club every Friday at 3 pm in the Oak Lounge has suggested that a few thoughts on the subject of singing would be timely in view of the interest in music generally, which is shown by the residents. Hence this article, in no particular chronological order.

Before departing from the mention of glee clubs, it is interesting to learn that originally 'glee' did not mean to sing joyfully, cheerfully, happily and other similar descriptions, but rather 'glee' was used as a noun, denoting a specific form of English seventeenth and eighteenth-century song. Glee clubs originated in England as choirs, generally of men but also of just women or mixed voices, which traditionally specialized in signing short songs. It seems there are few pure glee clubs still performing and most people have come to regard 'glee' in the adjectival sense. This is the case at Crofton Manor where we sing for joy.

Why, when and what do we sing? Speaking personally, I like to sing because I find rhythm and melody seem to come naturally and when combined with lyrics of different 'hues', they bring back memories or open horizons. For me, and I suspect many others, songs kindle nostalgic memories and/or hope for the future. As for when we sing, the answer is almost anytime from early morning ablutions — who doesn't sing in front of the basin, in the shower or in the bathtub? — and later during the day when devoid of other distractions, a song presents itself in our consciousness and maybe we burst into song, whistle or quietly hum to ourselves. Some people, mostly male constantly have a song in their hearts or on their lips ready to spring on long-suffering intimates, such as a romantic ballad to a wife or a lover or the object of his affection. The question of what we sing presents endless choices from world-famous classical music and operas to more modern-day sentimental melodies. Choice depends upon upbringing, education, and probably age and the era in which the individual lived. As a nonagenarian having lived through the Great Depression of the thirties and World War II, probably quite naturally I favour the swinging era of the big bands and, dare I say it, the great, often sentimental musical compositions played during the Lawrence Welk programs (which incidentally are still being broadcast weekly on the PBS TV network). I don't appreciate the modern rock music, probably because I don't understand it and also because I find it far too raucous. Admittedly, the whole question of choice boils down to *chacun à son gout.*

An aspect of singing lies in health effects. Singing is considered by some to have positive effects on peoples' health. A preliminary study based on self-reported data from a survey of students participating in choral singing found physical benefits, including increased lung capacity, improved mood and stress reduction, as well as social and spiritual benefits. Singing may positively influence the immune system through the reduction of stress. One study found that both singing and listening to choral music reduces the level of stress hormones and increases immune function. Certainly, it is reasonable at least to suggest that singing can do no harm unless one is addicted to listening to the yelling and screaming of some modern rockers who are supported by some equally noisy accompaniment. This I suspect probably produces patients for the hearing aid centres.

This article is, of course, about human song — but unlike laughter, which is confined to the human race, singing occurs in certain other species. These include birds and whales that produce a limited range of songs and could be the subject of another article.

Turning to the basics, as we are aware, singing is the act of producing musical sounds with the voice. It can be accompanied by a variety of musical instruments or 'a cappella', meaning without accompaniment. Generally speaking, anyone who can speak can sing. Singing can be informal and just for pleasure, such as at the aforementioned early morning ablution time, or it can be very formal, such as is done professionally. This latter usually requires a great deal of regular practice and instruction. Most top-flight performers receive training and instruction from voice coaches throughout their careers. A few

people are born with a 'gifted voice'. An interesting sta-
tistic out of England is that 16 people are born with such
voices each year, making 500 'first-class voices' active in
any particular generation.

Classical and operatic solo singers, are classified by
voice types measured by the *tessitura*, the vocal weight
and timbre of their voices. *Tessitura* by the way, is a noun
meaning the range within which most tones of a vocal
part fall.

Our Wonderful World of Idioms

by A. John Ellis

Is it any wonder that some non-English speakers trying to learn English become confused by our many idioms used in everyday conversation?

Take for instance the one of being "under the weather." Now I ask you, is there any logic to the idea of being "under the weather?" Many people use the idiom frequently without giving thought to the whys and wherefores of it, but knowing full well that it is readily recognized as meaning not feeling well or suffering some probably mild indisposition. I use the phrase regularly and it set me to thinking how did the idiom originate? A little research on the internet provided the surprising answer. This popular phrase for illness dates back to 1827 and is believed to have been originated by sailors. When they were sick, they would rest below deck and therefore were under the weather being experienced on deck! Think of the person trying to learn English faced with a sentence like "Ruth is the apple of her mother's eye, but she has a big chip on her shoulder probably because she is frequently under the weather." Perfectly comprehensible to us, containing three well-known idioms, but probably a very puzzling enigma to the foreigner who would find no logic or sense in a literal interpretation of the words themselves.

Following on the that chain of thought, I decided to research a few more of our commonly used idioms. So here goes, in the hope that you too may be interested in a brief look at what has given rise to some of the accepted English language idioms. As you may note, some date back to the Bible.

THE APPLE OF MY/HIS/HER/THEIR EYE.
This seems to hark back to Psalm 17, "A Prayer of David", which opens: "Hear the right, O Lord, attend unto my cry, give ear unto my prayer, that goeth not out of feigned lips", and there are 15 verses. Verse 8 reads: "Keep me as the apple of the eye, hide me under the shadow of thy wings."

BACK TO SQUARE ONE.
Meaning back to the beginning. This oft-used idiom was first heard on BBC soccer radio commentaries. Apparently, soccer action is difficult to describe on the radio so the announcers split the field into imaginary numbered squares so that listeners could be told where the ball was whenever the game

restarted after a break. Hence, "back to square one." I had always imagined it had something to do with drafting or engineering and perhaps you did too.

BLIND LEADING THE BLIND.

This is another common phrase, which means that the person in charge of a situation knows no more about it than those whom she/he is leading. It has biblical roots in Matthew 15:14. Jesus is reported to have said "Let them alone, they be blind leaders of the blind. And if the blind lead the blind, both shall fall into the ditch."

SHE/HE HAS A CHIP ON HIS/HER SHOULDER.

This means to carry a grudge and dates back to the 19th Century. A fighter would put a chip on his shoulder and dare antagonists to knock it off.

DEVIL'S ADVOCATE.

This actually comes from Canon Law. In the Vatican, when arguments are being presented to have a person declared a Saint, the Church looks to an official charged with the responsibility to find flaws in the evidence. He is titled the 'Devil's Advocate', which description is now used universally to mean a person who supports a cause just for the sake of argument.

YOU CAN'T TAKE IT WITH YOU.
This also is found in the Bible, in 1 Timothy
6:7. "For we brought nothing into this world,
and it is certain we carry nothing out."

There are countless idioms, with varied explanations, ranging from the ridiculous to the sublime. Suffice it to say that the refinement and expansion of languages and the creation of idioms have come a long way since prehistoric people existed.

Buncombe — Missouri Question

by A. John Ellis

'Buncombe' can also be spelled 'bunkum'. I know this because I emailed a facetious message to a family member, which I described as 'buncombe'. Having used the word for as long as I can remember, it suddenly dawned on me that I hadn't the faintest idea of its origin. *Webster's New Twentieth Century Dictionary of the English Language (unabridged)* states as follows:

> buncombe — *bunkum* N — anything said for mere show, inflated or bombastic speechmaking, or for the gratification of constituents or to gain applause, empty talk

The word originated near the close of the debate on the Missouri Question in the sixteenth US Congress. Felix Walker, an old North Carolina mountaineer whose district included the County of Buncombe, rose to speak. Several members begged him to desist, but he persevered, declaring that his constituents expected it and he was bound to talk for Buncombe. So, apparently he got up and delivered an unwanted empty talk. From then on, the dictionary word for empty talk has been 'buncombe'/'bunkum'.

Having settled the matter of the origin of the word, I next realized that, while vaguely aware of the Missouri Question, I did not really know its importance or implications. It seems in the early 1800s, there was a growing awareness that slavery was an iniquity, which should be eliminated. Missouri, favouring slavery, was at the centre of the debate that at times was fierce, only to wane at other times with suggested compromises. Eventually, it led to the disastrous civil war.

The Missouri Question was all about the abolition or continuation of slavery. The South wanted to continue to benefit from cheap labour, which the slaves provided, while the North wanted everyone to enjoy freedom and the good life offered in America.

An extract from the Jefferson Encyclopedia gives an inkling of this horrendous problem facing the states.

In December 1819, ex-US president John Adams made a hand-wringing statement:

> The banks, bankrupt law, manufactures, Spanish treaty are nothing. These are occurrences, which like waves in a storm will pass under the ship. But the Missouri Question is a breaker on which we lose the Missouri country by revolt, and what's more, God only knows, from the Battle of Bunker's Hill, to the

> treaty of Paris, we never had so ominous a
> question. I thank God that I shall not live to
> witness its issue.

His fears were well-founded, as history has proven.

In the North, there were suggestions that the slaves should be freed and resettled in Africa, which led to the founding of Liberia. The Virginia legislature debated the abolition of slavery in 1829 and 1831. The furor over the matter had seemed to have quieted down somewhat during the 1820s, but even so, between 1776 and 1860, there were some 200-slave uprisings. One of the bloodiest, which struck fear in many white residences, occurred in 1831. Nat Turner and a few slaves rebelled in Virginia. They moved about the farming district, killing whites and recruiting more slaves for their crusade. About eighty slaves were involved in the end and they killed sixty whites before the militia finally put down the revolt. The uprising caused some southerners to advocate abolition but they were outnumbered by their greedy peers. In Philadelphia, the American Anti-Slavery Society was founded, which grew to 1,350 chapters with in excess of 250,000 members dedicated to freeing the slaves.

The movement smouldered until the spring of 1861, when the U.S. Civil War erupted between the North and the South. Sadly, a great nation divided, with massive devastation in its wake. The conflict terminated in May of 1865 and the nation was reunited. Over 620,000 Americans died in the war, with disease killing twice as many as those killed in battle. Fifty thousand survivors were amputees.

In 1936, Margaret Mitchell authored the best-selling novel of its time, entitled *Gone with the Wind*. Well-written, it is a gripping and most interesting account of the Civil War, a must-read. An excellent motion picture adaptation was produced well over sixty years ago starring Vivien Leigh and Clark Gable. Both book and film are still popular.

In spite of the carnage and devastation, the conflict was not in vain. Witness the many African-American descendants of the slaves today who, with the benefit of education, are successfully competing and making their marks in most fields of endeavour. They excel in the arts as musicians and entertainers. They are holding down top government posts from mayors to Secretary of State. In the sporting world, black athletes dominate in basketball and football. And who hasn't heard of Tiger Woods, the world-class golfer? Who in those days of battle could have imagined a black president, a promise fulfilled by Barack Obama?

So, perhaps the old adage "it's an ill wind that blows nobody any good" applies here as far as race distinction is concerned. That's no 'buncombe', or if you prefer, 'bunkum'. And thank you, Felix Walker, for being the cause of giving us such a useful and descriptive word.

The Order of Canada

by A. John Ellis

The Order of Canada is the keystone of our country's system of honours. It is the highest recognition Canada gives to the citizens and pays tribute to Canadians who exemplify the highest qualities of citizenship and whose contributions enrich the lives of their contemporaries. The Latin motto of this recognition of merit — *desiderantes meliorem patriam* — proclaims the aspirations of its members who, in their lives and work have shown that "they desire a better country."

Since its creation on July 1st, 1967, through to August 7th 2008, there have been 5,553 awards made to nominees, of whom 3,205 are still living. Canada's population in early August 2008 was estimated to total around 33,341,700 people, so the percentage of those who have been awarded the Order is extremely tiny (actually 0.0166%). Hence, those charged with the responsibility of determining the eligibility of the nominees must do so with great diligence, which they have been doing conscientiously over the years. Recently, there has been a storm of letters written to the press as a result of an award made to Dr. Morgenthaler — some favourable, others critical and many, I consider, unfairly castigating the Order per se. To my knowledge, in the 41-year history of the Order, there has never been such a volume of comments made over an appointee. In fact, I do not recall any previous public critiques of an appointment made of the Order, which I think you will agree, speaks well for the selection process of some 5,550 other appointments since the Order's inauguration. There have been two instances of orders being revoked after thorough investigation of the individuals' behavior. One of those provoked a lot of public indignation at the slowness to act but, following warranted due diligence, the administrators took the proper step.

It seems to me that, understandably, the general public has scant knowledge of most aspects of the Order and, with the thought that a description of its founding and operation might be of interest to you, I'll endeavour to set out the salient facts.

The reason the Order was established was because the government wanted a distinctively Canadian honours system without titles since knighthood appointments, previously made by the Queen/King of England, were not something the government felt should be part of our society.

Three levels of membership in the Order were established and designed to embrace a spectrum of achievement and service. These are:

- Companion (C.C.)
- Officer (O.C)
- Member (C.M)

The Companion recognizes outstanding achievement and merit of the highest degree, especially in service to Canada or to humanity at large.

The Officer, achievement and merit of a high degree, especially service to Canada or to humanity at large.

The Member award is made for distinguished service in or to a particular community, group or field of activity.

Other than the right to use post-nominal letters and to wear the insignia of the Order, membership gives no special privileges and no monetary reward. The number of new members each year is limited to 15 Companions, 64 Officers and 136 Members. The maximum allowable number of living Companions is 165. The breakdown of the membership as of August 7, 2008 was:

- Companion   163
- Officer   1015
- Member   2027

The constitution in part states that the Order of Canada shall consist of Her Majesty in right of Canada, the Governor General of Canada, who shall be the Chancellor and the Companions, Officers and Members and the honorary Companions, Officers and Members. The Chancellor is responsible for the administration of the Order and the Secretary to the GG shall be the Secretary General of the Order with all the usual duties on which I shan't elaborate.

The particularly important body is the Council, which meets regularly and has the final say on appointments to the Order. It consists of:

- The Chief Justice of Canada who acts as Chair of the Council
- The Clerk of the Privy Council
- The Deputy Minister of the Department of Canadian Heritage
- The Chair of the Canada Council
- The President of the Royal Society of Canada
- The Chair of the Board of Directors of the Association of Universities and Colleges of Canada

Also, the Governor General may, on the recommendation of the above-mentioned Council Members, appoint five persons belonging to the Order as members of the Council for a three-year term.

Any Canadian citizen may be appointed to the Order and any person or organization may submit to the Secretary General for consideration by the Council a nomination of a Canadian citizen for appointment to the Order. A person who is not a Canadian citizen may be appointed as an honorary Companion, Officer or Member.

There is a great deal more that could be written about the Order of Canada and its constitution, but hopefully the foregoing indicates that it is indeed a worthy institution, well-constituted and administered by a group of outstanding Canadians. From the statistics shown, it is apparent that their 'batting average' would be the envy of any baseball league!

John receiving an honorary doctorate at Simon Fraser University in 1992.

Canadian Embassy in Japan, 1992.

John and Joan with Peter Lougheed.

John and family members on the occasion of a dedication for the "A. John Ellis Team Room" at the SFU Segal Graduate School of Business on September 6th, 2007.

John cutting the ceremonial ribbon for the dedication of the "Team Room", 2007.

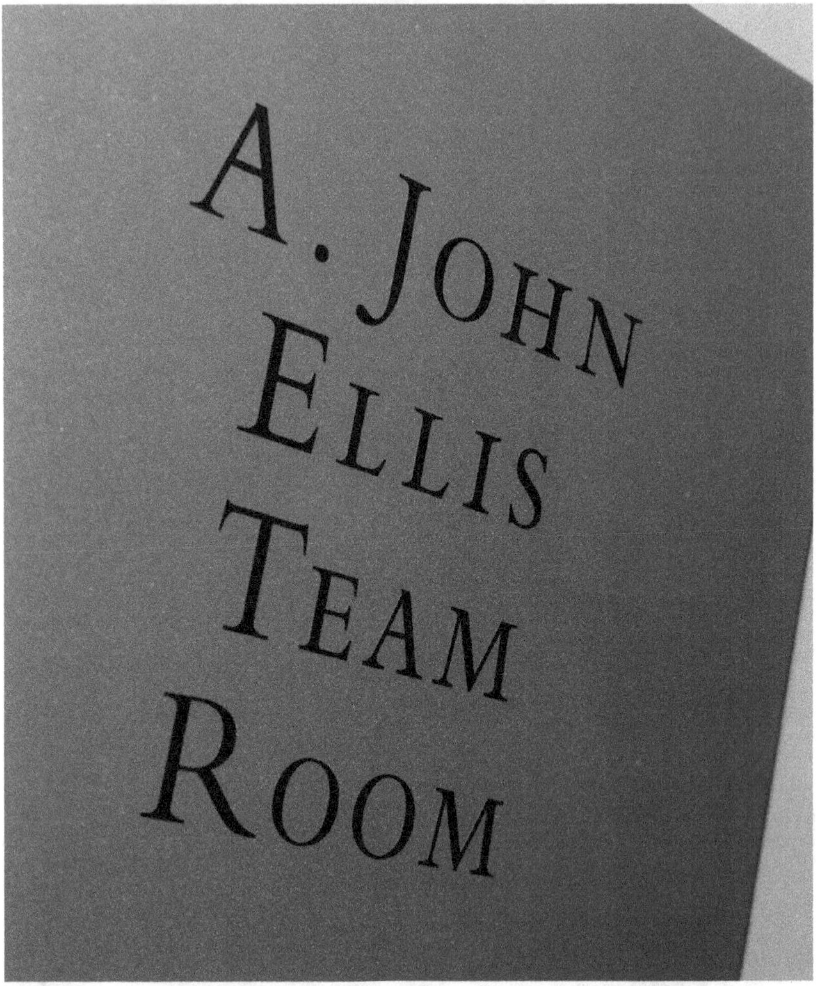
A. John
Ellis
Team
Room

Convocation and procession at SFU.

John addressing attendees on the day of his Team Room dedication at SFU.

John, Susan and Joan at the 65th wedding dinner celebration.

Left to right: Severin, Susan, John and a friend preparing to entertain Crofton Manor residents.

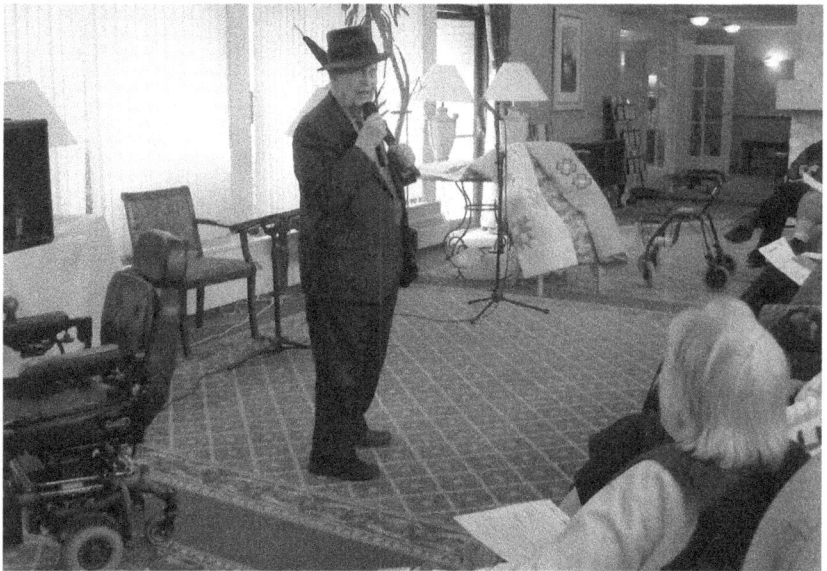

John shows he's not afraid of performing in front of an audience.

John addresses guests at his 100th birthday party.

John with MBA students who have been recipients of his scholarship.

Robert Ellis, son of John.

The Bank of Montreal branch in the Bentall complex near the Burrard Skytrain Station. To the left is BMO's main office building, where John served as Vice-Chairman of the board.

Still connecting with friends and colleagues at BMO annual meeting in Toronto, 2014. John with his old friend Ray Moriyama, world-famous architect.

Curriculum Vitae
A. John Ellis
OC, ORS, LLD (Honourary)

A. John Ellis, Order of Canada, 1983, Order of The Rising Sun (from Emperor of Japan as authorized by special Order-in Council, Ottawa), 1989, LLD (Honoris Causa) from Simon Fraser University, 1992.

A financial entrepreneur and long-time banker serving with the Bank of Montreal from coast to coast and internationally. Retired as Vice-Chairman of the Board in 1975, Director 1973-1986 and presently an Honorary Director. Past Director and/or Chairman of numerous diverse companies in Canada, USA and Japan. Chair for fifteen years of Marsh & McLennan Advisory Board. Past Chair of NIM Management Ltd., which at one time funded 50% of Canadian mining explorations. Served several years with the Canadian Institute of Chartered Accountants on their Account Research Advisory Board and as a member of their Special Committee on Standard Setting (SCOSS).

Active in community affairs throughout his career, including Chair and now Governor of the Canadian Chamber of Commerce (170,000 members); past President of Douglas Hospital in Verdun, Quebec (one of Canada's largest mental health hospitals); past Chairman and subsequently Hon. Chair & Director Emeritus of Canada Development Corporation, Past Gen Campaign Chair of the United Appeals in Halifax, NS and in Vancouver. Past President and now Hon. VP and Hon. Member Canada-Japan Society of B.C. Past Chair and/or Director numerous community organizations such as Canadian Red Cross, Heart & Stroke Foundation of BC & Yukon, Vancouver Playhouse Theatre, Pacific Basin Economic Council Canadian Committee, Endeavour and others. A total of 36 boards and committees as a Chairman and/or Director.

Convocation Founder, Member of Senate Simon Fraser University and major fund raiser for SFU, UVic and and UBC. Director for six years of Banff School of Advanced Management.

Five years with Canadian Armed Forces serving in Canada, England and North West Europe.

He and his wife travelled extensively throughout Canada and internationally on business speaking en-gagements and attending bi-lateral and multilateral associations' meetings.

To this day, he continues to attend the annual general meeting of the Bank of Montreal in Toronto. The only one he missed, was when he turned 100, but he did make it when he was 101. His goal is to attend it on the bank's 200th anniversary. He'll be 102 then.

www.ingramcontent.com/pod-product-compliance
Lightning Source LLC
Chambersburg PA
CBHW060046100426
42742CB00014B/2714